ACKNOWLEDGMENTS

My husband BILL - I know without doubt I couldn't have done this book as quickly and easily if you weren't by my side. Thank you for believing in me and loving me as you do. A special thank you for your help with the photo shoot, your talent with the food styling was incredible.

My daughters KELLIE, RACHEL and JENNA - Thank you for once again putting up with the never ending cooking and taste testing. As I watch you girls grow into the wonderful women that you are my heart is filled with so much pride and love. You are my number one cheer squad and I love you girls so much. A special mention to Kellie who is my Office Assistant, thanks for your help in running the office, we make a great team.

My mum FAY - I am so grateful for your love and support. I treasure our time together and the close relationship that we share. My sister LEONIE who is such a caring person. You are my confidant, my friend and above all a treasured sister. My sister LINDA who is such a sweetie and so much fun to be with. We have a special relationship that I value greatly. LINDA I can't thank you enough for thinking of the title SYMPLY TOO GOOD TO BE TRUE, you are so clever. My mother and father in-law SHIRLEY and BILL - I will never forget the help you gave me when I first started and your continued support.

Photographer ALISON - CHILLI DESIGN. Thank you for making such an arduous task so easy and above all fun. You did a fantastic job, well done. Ph: Alison (07) 5437 7788.

Dietitian LISA COCHRANE - Thank you so much for your advice, knowledge and expertise. Thank you for all you contributed to help make this book so fabulous.

Printer - THE INK SPOT PRINTERS. JOHN, CHRISTINE, IAN and TEAM, thank you for all the support you have given me over the years. You have been with me from the start and always do an outstanding job, book 5 is no exception. Well done! Ph: (07) 5443 5431.

Graphics - CHILLI DESIGN. Thank you DARREN, NATALIE and team. I love what you have done with this new book. A great effort from a very talented team. Ph: (07) 5437 7788.

Myer, Maroochydore - KERRY, KATH, TODD and ELIZABETH. Thank you for your help. All home ware products used in this book were provided courtesy of Myer. To contact your nearest Myer store please call 1800 811 611.

Distributors - NETWORK SERVICES. NEIL, ZOE and WIL. Thank you for distributing thousands upon thousands of my cookbooks all over Australia and doing it as well as you do. A special thank you to my past account manager GRACE.

Proofreaders - LEONIE, FIONA, LEETA, VICKI and MICHELLE. Final proofing done by BRYAN WARD thewritestuffinoz@hotmail.com. Thank you all for doing such a terrific job.

Taste testers - KELLIE, RACHEL, JENNA, CHRIS, THE BREKICH FAMILY, THE KASTEEL FAMILY, THE PARKER FAMILY, BEV, BUD, BEBE, STUART, KIM, WAYNE, BRENT, MICHELLE and RYAN. A big thanks to you all for helping critique my recipes. Without your opinions this book would not have been as fabulous as it is.

To my family and friends - I have a small but special family, thank you to the Sym side of the family, for your support over the years. I am especially proud of my nieces and nephews who I love and adore. I could not imagine my life without my best friends Kath, Kim, Jan and Vicki. You are family to me and I love you all to bits, you are my best friends in the whole world. Our dear friends BEBE and STUART thank you for your support over the years. A special mention to Chris my future son-in-law, you are such a special man and I am so glad you are marrying my Rachel.

Finally to all the people who have one or more of my cookbooks, I can't thank you enough for valuing what I do. If you have lost weight, gained better health or discovered the joy of cooking through my cookbooks then I am one happy lady.

Thank you everyone from the bottom of my healthy heart.

CONT[ENTS]

DEDICATION - I would like to dedicate this book to my wonderful husband Bill. We celebrated our 32nd wedding anniversary this year (2006) and I want you to know that I love you more now than ever before. Bill you are not only my husband but also my best friend. You have made me feel so special and that I can achieve anything I want to with you proudly standing by my side. You are my everything and I want to thank you for being such a wonderful father to our three girls and for looking after us so well. You are an amazing man and I love you more than words can say. You are my hero.

Welcome Back...

The old Annette at 100 kilos and a healthy Annette at 65 kilos.

Here is SYMPLY TOO GOOD TO BE TRUE 5. I have had so much fun writing and creating this very special book and have filled it with some incredibly delicious 'guilt-free' recipes, that I am sure your whole family will enjoy. My mission was to once again create a cookbook as good as my other four. Not an easy task but to be honest I believe book 5 is the best yet. There are all new and delicious recipes for you to try in this book and as always they are quick and easy to make, with all the ingredients available in supermarkets.

For those of you who are new to my cookbooks, in a nutshell I lost 35 kilos in 20 months and have maintained my healthy weight for many years. I was a chubby child, cuddly teenager, buxom bride and for many years an obese adult. After losing my weight everyone kept asking for my recipes and encouraged me to put them into a book, and the rest, as they say, is history. My cookbooks have helped thousands of people to become healthy and still have the food they enjoy.

I have a forum on my website www.symplytoogood.com.au where people can chat to other like-minded people about anything to do with cooking, health and wellbeing. It was interesting reading the many suggestions people posted on what they wanted to see in book 5. One suggestion that kept coming up time and time again was sandwich ideas. So you asked for it, and you got it. If you are sick of cheese and tomato sandwiches, then rest assured you now have many symple, tasty and healthy ideas in the new section called SANDWICH FILLINGS.

Another new addition to SYMPLY TOO GOOD TO BE TRUE 5 is my 28-DAY WEIGHT LOSS PLAN. People say they just don't know what to eat or how much they should be eating to lose weight, so this plan will help get you started and by following the 28-day plan you will learn the healthy way to shed kilos. If you need a kick start or have an important event coming up, how great is it to now have a four-week plan to help you knock those kilos off. With the support and advice of dietitian Lisa Cochrane I was able to put together what I believe is a fantastic weight loss plan. Not only does

this plan meet the Australian Dietary requirements, it is so healthy that it is suitable for people with diabetes. So get started and say goodbye to your excess weight. For more info on the planner please go to the Weight Loss Menu Plan Information. Also if, after the 28 days, you want more menu planning support, why not consider my SYMPLY TOO GOOD TO BE TRUE CD-Rom Menu Planner.

On a personal note, since launching my fourth cookbook, I have had some very exciting times. Winning the Australian Telstra Micro Business of the Year in 2004 was a major highlight. I was also proud to be listed in BRW Magazine's 2006 list of Australia's top 50 entrepreneurial women. I came in at number 27. But, what fills me up with joy more than anything else are the people who I meet who say how much they value what I do. Check out the testimonial section and you will see what I mean. How fabulous are all these wonderful people who have taken the time to write, email or call me to tell me how much they are enjoying my recipes.

I hope you enjoy my new book and happy cooking.

Enjoy Every Mouthful!

BRANDS THAT I USED IN THIS BOOK - All stock powder used are Massel. Soup mixes and 4 Cheese sauce - Continental.

FREEZING RECIPES - To make it easier for you I have included a symbol at the top right hand corner of every nutritional panel.

 THIS SYMBOL MEANS IT IS SUITABLE TO BE FROZEN

 THIS SYMBOL MEANS IT IS NOT SUITABLE TO BE FROZEN.

FOR CORRECT MEASUREMENTS

In every recipe a metric measuring cup and spoon were used. For example, the tablespoon I have used equals 15g. If you were using a metal tablespoon be aware that it could measure from 20 to 30g a spoon. I didn't use a tea cup - when I say 1 cup of flour, I have used a 250ml measuring cup as shown.

The adjustable teaspoon and tablespoon can be purchased from my website:
www.symplytoogood.com.au or Ph 07 5445 1250

28 Day Weight Loss Plan Introduction

This 28-day weight loss plan has been devised to assist anyone who wants to lose weight the healthy way. So many times people say that dieting is too hard, that they don't know what to eat and how much to have. Some diets are also unhealthy and boring, but my plan will show you how you can lose weight and still have delicious food including the occasional treat. This is such a healthy plan that it is suitable for people with diabetes. Just follow each day and enjoy the plan, it's that simple!

With a balance of carbohydrates over the day, you will find that you won't get the energy highs and lows that normal dieting gives. It also uses some of the fabulous recipes found in SYMPLY TOO GOOD TO BE TRUE 5, so you will find it easy to create the meals required. You can also make most of the recipes up ahead of time and freeze them so you can then have the convenience of preparing the week ahead if you need to. By following this plan you will have enough calcium, fibre, carbohydrates and protein each day, all balanced with a low saturated fat diet.

This 28-day menu plan is not suitable for children, pregnant or breastfeeding women.

You can lose weight by just following this plan, but it is highly recommended that you also include a minimum of 20 minutes physical activity, most days of the week.

All menus have been reviewed and approved by Lisa Cochrane, Senior Dietitian, Diabetes Australia - Victoria. The book has also been endorsed nationally by Diabetes Australia. The 28-day menu plan meets the recommendations of the Dietary Guidelines for Australian Adults. Please consult your doctor before embarking on this 28-day plan or any diet.

LISA COCHRANE'S COMMENT: People with diabetes will benefit from this 28-day menu plan, which provides them with examples of how to incorporate healthy recipes into their entire eating plan. Unlike many weight management and diabetes menu plans, Annette has included the occasional not so healthy food into the menus, making this diet realistic and potentially maintainable over a long period of time. Annette has also included snacks that are low in fat and contain moderate amounts of carbohydrate. These can be included at morning tea, afternoon tea or supper. However, it is recommended that people with diabetes distribute the snacks at two snack times rather than having one large snack. This will help to maintain stable blood glucose levels. Through having 3 healthy low joule meals a day, 2 snacks and incorporating some physical activity in their day, people with diabetes have a great opportunity to achieve a long, complication free life.

WHICH LEVEL SHOULD YOU BE ON?

LEVEL 1 -
· If you want quick weight loss
· Have only a few kilos to lose
· Do not do any exercise
· Are a senior and not very mobile
· If you have a slow metabolism.

LEVEL 2 -
· If you have 15 or more kilos to lose
· If you are a very active female
· If you are an inactive man.

WHAT IS THE DIFFERENCE BETWEEN LEVEL 1 AND LEVEL 2?

LEVEL 1 - For a woman who is inactive or has less than 10 kilos to lose. The average daily allowance is around 30g of fat and 5500 kilojoules (1300 cals). If you have only a few kilos to lose it will be important that you follow the plan exactly as is and include exercise.

LEVEL 1 - You must eat what is listed for BREAKFAST, LUNCH, DINNER AND SNACKS IN LEVEL 1 ONLY for each day. You do not get the extra section on LEVEL 2.

LEVEL 2 - For a woman who is reasonably active or who has more than 15 kilos to lose. It would also be suitable for an inactive man. The average daily allowance is around 40g of fat and 6500 kilojoules (1600 cals).

LEVEL 2 - You must eat what is listed for BREAKFAST, LUNCH, DINNER AND SNACKS in LEVEL 1 plus what is listed in the LEVEL 2 section for each day.

Don't miss any of the food listed as it may cause you to be hungry the following day. Don't swap any choices from one day to another and only eat what is on the list for that day. Eating more than what is listed on the daily menu may jeopardise your weight loss.

SALAD AND VEGETABLES: Salad and vegetables are unlimited but have at least what is suggested in the menu. Salad consists of lettuce, tomato, cucumber, capsicum, onion, sprouts, beetroot, celery, carrot. It does not include avocado or corn.

Vegetables means all vegetables except potato, sweet potato and corn. If you are to have any of these choices they will be listed separately.

CEREALS: 9 grain bread and multi grain bread rolls are used due to their lower GI rating. Rice should be Basmati rice as it too has a lower GI rating.

If you have a gluten or wheat intolerance replace bread with gluten free bread that weighs no more than 36g a slice and replace pasta with rice pasta. Make sure that the other ingredients in the recipe are also gluten free.

DRINKS: Use the skim milk allocated in the snacks section for tea and coffee or as a drink. If you are lactose intolerant then use no-fat soy milk. Have only a couple of cups of coffee or tea each day unless they are de-caffeinated. De-caffeinated diet soft drinks are allowed.

Alcohol is not included in the menus. If you wish to include alcohol be aware that you are adding extra kilojoules to your day, which may slow your weight loss down.

Drink at least 8 glasses of water every day.

TIPS: Don't guess the weights of food such as 120g chicken. I would suggest you invest in a small set of digital scales so your portions are accurate. If you do not want one of the choices that are from BOOK 5 then check the kilojoules and fat count of that recipe per serve, and if you wish you can swap it for another recipe from any of the Symply Too Good To Be True cookbooks. Make sure that the recipe you choose has a similar fat and kilojoule count, otherwise it will alter the balance of the day.

28-Day Weight Loss Plan - Weeks 1 and 2

		Day 1	Day 2	Day 3
LEVEL 1	**Breakfast**	3 Weet-bix ¾ cup skim milk 1 cup canned peaches (no sugar added) drained	3 Weet-bix ¾ cup skim milk 1 medium size fruit	¾ cup cooked (30g raw) rolled oats made with water ½ cup skim milk 2 slices fruit toast 1 tsp Flora Light margarine
	Lunch	1 50g multi grain bread roll 50g cooked chicken breast no skin 1½ cups salad 1 tsp 97% ff mayonnaise 140g kiwi fruit	2 slices 9 grain bread 30g sliced deli turkey 1 slice Bega Super Slim cheese 1½ cups salad 1 tsp 97% ff mayonnaise ¾ cup canned peaches (no sugar added) drained 20g raw almonds	½ serve Chinese Omelette BOOK 5 _P20_ 1 cup salad 1 medium size fruit 1 Weight Watchers Fruit Duo Cereal Bar
	Dinner	1 serve Curry in a Hurry BOOK 5 _P 37_ ¾ cup cooked Basmati rice	✱1 serve Tuna Patties BOOK 5 2 cups vegetables or salad 1 serve Berry Dream BOOK 5 ✱ p. 31	125g cooked lean roast pork 100g potato baked with cooking spray 125g pumpkin baked with cooking spray 1 small onion baked with — cooking spray / 1 cup vegetables / ¼ cup low joule gravy (Gravox) / ¾ cup canned peaches (no added sugar) drained
	Snacks	1 cup skim milk 1 serve Berry Dream BOOK 5 1 All Bran baked bar _p62_	½ cup skim milk 2 Ryvita crispbreads 1 tsp Flora Light margarine 2 tsps jam 1 serve Chocolate Slice BOOK 5 _p69_	1 cup skim milk 1 x 200g diet fruit yoghurt 1 slice Apple Prune Loaf BOOK 5 _p68_
LEVEL 2	**Extras**	LUNCH - 30g avocado DINNER - ¼ cup more rice SNACK - 30g lite Cadbury milk chocolate	LUNCH - 1 extra tsp margarine DINNER - 1 extra tuna patty SNACK - 20g more raw almonds	SNACKS - 30g dry roasted unsalted cashews, 1 medium size fruit

		Day 8	Day 9	Day 10
LEVEL 1	**Breakfast**	1 slice 9 grain bread toasted ½ cup canned spaghetti in tomato & cheese sauce 1 medium size fruit	1 cup Wheatbran Flakes Bodysmart ½ cup skim milk ¾ cup canned peaches (no sugar added) drained	2 slices fruit toast 2 tsps Flora Light margarine 125g kiwi fruit
	Lunch	1 serve Thai Beef Noodle salad BOOK 5 _p17_ 1 Uncle Toby's Crunchy Apricot Muesli Bar ¾ cup canned peaches (no sugar added) drained	1 50g multi grain bread roll 1 slice Bega Super Slim cheese 20g sliced 97% ff ham 1½ cups salad 1 medium size fruit	1 lavash bread 30g 25% reduced fat tasty cheese 1½ cups salad 30g avocado
	Dinner	100g raw chicken sausage (Leonards) grilled 100g potato 1 cup cooked English spinach 1 serve Vegetable Crumble BOOK 5	1 serve Spaghetti Bake BOOK 5 2 cups salad _p45_	1 serve Fish Bruschetta BOOK 5 2 cups vegetables or salad 1 x 125g Fromage Frais Light Fruche _p32_
	Snacks	1 cup skim milk 200g fresh strawberries 1 Weight Watchers Fruit Duo Cereal Bar	1 cup skim milk 1 All Bran baked bar 1 x 200g diet fruit yoghurt	1 cup skim milk 1 medium size fruit 1 Berry Nice Slice BOOK 5 _p66_
LEVEL 2	**Extras**	SNACKS - 1 extra medium size fruit, 1 Lite Mars Bar	SNACKS - 25g raw almonds, 1 medium size fruit	SNACK - 1 x 50g pkt corn chips

Day 4	Day 5	Day 6	Day 7
½ cup All Bran cereal ¾ cup skim milk 1 medium size fruit	¾ cup Wheatbran Flakes Bodysmart ½ cup skim milk 1 cup canned peaches (no sugar added) drained	1 slice 9 grain bread toasted ½ cup baked beans 1 small tomato 40g mushrooms 1 medium size fruit	¾ cup Wheatbran Flakes Bodysmart ½ cup skim milk 1 medium size fruit
1 Four 'n' Twenty Lite Meat Pie 1 tsp tomato sauce 1 medium size fruit	4 Ryvita crispbreads 1 slice Bega Super Slim cheese 20g 97% ff ham 1½ cups salad 2 tsps Flora Light margarine 1 medium size fruit	2 slices 9 grain bread 60g Roast Pork from Day 3 dinner 1½ cups salad 1 x 200g diet fruit yoghurt	1 Caesar Toasted Sandwich BOOK 5 *p56* 1 x 200g diet fruit yoghurt
1 serve Stuffed Apricot Chicken BOOK 5 *p40* 2 cups vegetables or salad	1 serve Crumbed Fish with Cheese Sauce BOOK 5 *p34* ¾ cup cooked Basmati rice 2 cups vegetables or salad	1 serve Chicken Crumble BOOK 5 *p39* 100g potato skin on 1 cup vegetables	1 x 175g Four 'n' Twenty Lite Meat Pie 100g potato 2 cups vegetables or salad
1 cup skim milk 2 Cruskit crispbreads 2 slices Bega Super Slim cheese 1 small tomato 1 slice Apple Prune Loaf BOOK 5 *p68*	1 cup skim milk 1 x 200g diet fruit yoghurt 25g raw almonds	1 cup skim milk 2 Cruskit crispbreads 1 slice Bega Super Slim cheese 1 tsp Flora Light margarine ½ tsp Vegemite 1 medium size fruit	1 cup skim milk 200g fresh strawberries 1 Weight Watchers Fruit Duo Cereal Bar
SNACK - 50g Red Rock Deli Chips	SNACKS - 10g more raw almonds, 4 Pikelets BOOK 5, 1 tsp Flora Light margarine, 1 tsp jam	LUNCH - 30g more cooked roast pork, 1 tsp Flora Light margarine. DINNER - 50g more potato SNACK - 2 more Cruskits, 1 slice Bega Super Slim cheese, ½ tsp more Vegemite, 1 tsp Flora Light margarine	SNACK - 50g Red Rock Deli Chips

Day 11	Day 12	Day 13	Day 14
1 multi grain English muffin toasted 1 slice Bega Super Slim cheese 1 small tomato	1 slice 9 grain bread toasted ½ cup canned spaghetti tomato & cheese sauce 1 tomato grilled 1 tsp Flora Light margarine 1 medium size fruit	1 Weight Watchers Fruit Duo Cereal Bar 1 medium size fruit	1 fruit smoothie (using 1 cup skim milk and 1 medium size fruit) 1 round crumpet 1 tsp Flora Light margarine 1 tsp honey
4 Cruskit crispbreads 80g pink salmon drained 2 cups salad 1 tsp Flora Light margarine 150g kiwi fruit	1 Roast Beef & Chutney Sandwich BOOK 5 *p52* 1 cup salad 1 medium size fruit	1 50g multi grain bread roll 30g 25% reduced fat tasty cheese 1½ cups salad 1 tsp 97% ff mayonnaise 1 x 200g diet fruit yoghurt	2 Tacos BOOK 5 *p18* 25g avocado 1 medium size fruit
1 Satay Pork Burger BOOK 5, including bun and salad *p43* 1 extra cup salad 100g potato - cut in chips, coat with cooking spray and bake in oven.	1 serve Roast Pumpkin & Spinach Pie BOOK 5 *p25* 125g potato 2 cups vegetables or salad 1 tub Diet Choc Mousse (Nestle)	1 serve Ginger Lime Fish BOOK 5 *p33* ¾ cup cooked rice 2 cups vegetables or salad 20g raw almonds	1 serve Beef Goulash BOOK 5 ¾ cup cooked pasta 1 cup vegetables or salad
1 cup skim milk 1 All Bran baked bar 1 x 125g Fromage Frais Light Fruche	¾ cup skim milk 1 Uncle Toby's Crunchy Apricot Muesli Bar 2 Ryvita crispbreads 1 tsp Flora Light margarine 1 slice Bega Super Slim cheese ½ tsp Vegemite	1 cup skim milk 200g fresh strawberries 1 slice Berry Nice Slice BOOK 5 *p68*	1 cup skim milk 1 Weight Watchers Duo Fruit Cereal Bar 2 Ryvita crispbreads 1 tsp Flora Light margarine 1 tsp Vegemite
LUNCH - 25g 25% reduced fat tasty cheese DINNER - 75g more potato SNACK - 1 chocolate Paddle Pop	LUNCH - 20g raw almonds DINNER - extra ½ serve Pumpkin & Spinach Pie	SNACKS - 1 chocolate Paddle Pop, 20g more raw almonds	LUNCH - 1 extra taco, 25g more avocado DINNER - ¼ cup more cooked pasta

28 Day Weight Loss Plan - Weeks 3 and 4

		Day 15	Day 16	Day 17
LEVEL 1	**Breakfast**	2 slices 9 grain bread toasted 1 tsp Flora Light margarine 1 tsp Vegemite 1 x 125g pear	¾ cup cooked (30g raw) rolled oats made with water ½ cup skim milk 10g sultanas	3 Weet-bix 1 cup skim milk 1 cup canned peaches (no sugar added) drained
	Lunch	1 50g multi grain bread roll 1 slice Bega Super Slim cheese 1 tsp 97% ff mayonnaise 1½ cups salad 1 x 125g orange	1 serve Roast Pumpkin & Spinach Pie BOOK 5 *p 25* 1½ cups salad 30g avocado 1 medium size fruit	1 Chilli Beef & Salad Sandwich BOOK 5 1 medium size fruit
	Dinner	½ tub Latina Bolognaise 1 cup cooked pasta 2 cups salad 1 tsp grated parmesan cheese	1 serve Chicken Cordon Bleu BOOK 5 100g potato, skin on 2 cups vegetables or salad ½ cup low fat custard	2 pieces I & J Crumbed Lite Lemon fish 125g new potatoes, skin on 2 cups vegetables or salad 1 x 200g diet fruit yoghurt
	Snacks	1 cup skim milk 1 x 200g diet fruit yoghurt 1 All Bran baked bar	¾ cup skim milk 1 medium size fruit 4 Ryvita crispbreads 1 tsp Flora Light margarine 1 tsp Vegemite 1 tsp peanut butter	¾ cup skim milk 25g raw almonds 1 Uncle Toby's Crunchy Apricot Muesli Bar
LEVEL 2	**Extras**	SNACK - 1 50g pkt corn chips	LUNCH - 1 (50g) multigrain bread roll, 1 tsp Flora Light margarine, 30g more avocado	DINNER - 1 extra piece of crumbed fish SNACK - 1 extra medium fruit & 10g more raw almonds

		Day 22	Day 23	Day 24
LEVEL 1	**Breakfast**	1 English fruit muffin 1 tsp Flora Light margarine 1 medium size fruit	½ cup All Bran cereal ¾ cup skim milk 1 cup canned peaches (no sugar added) drained	¾ cup All Bran cereal ¾ cup skim milk 1 medium size fruit
	Lunch	2 slices 9 grain bread 1 boiled egg 1 tsp 97% ff mayonnaise ½ cup shredded lettuce ¾ cup canned pineapple in natural juice drained	1 Caesar Toasted Sandwich BOOK 5 1 medium size fruit	2 slices 9 grain bread 30g 25% reduced fat tasty cheese 1½ cups salad 2 tsps 97% ff mayonnaise 1x 125g Fromage Frais Light Fruche
	Dinner	125g raw fish fillet (cook with cooking spray in non stick frypan) 1 serve Italian Potatoes BOOK 5 2 cups vegetables or salad 1 x 200g diet fruit yoghurt	1 serve Chinese Beef BOOK 5 ¾ cup cooked Basmati rice 1 x 200g diet fruit yoghurt	1 serve Mexican Chicken Stack BOOK 5 *p40* 1 cup extra salad 30g avocado 1 medium size fruit
	Snacks	1½ cups skim milk 1 slice Apricot and Walnut Loaf BOOK 5 *p69* 2 Ryvita crispbreads 1 tablespoon peanut butter	1 cup skim milk 35g dried apricots 2 Ryvita crispbreads 50g avocado 1 small tomato	¾ cup skim milk 1 x 135g fruit Snack Pack 1 slice Chocolate Slice BOOK 5 *p68*
LEVEL 2	**Extras**	DINNER - Add 25g more raw fish, extra ½ serve Italian Potatoes. SNACK - 25g unsalted cashews	DINNER - add ½ cup more cooked rice SNACK - 20g raw almonds	LUNCH - 2 tsps Flora Light Margarine SNACKS - 1 extra medium fruit, 1 x 20g snack size potato chips

Day 18	Day 19	Day 20	Day 21
1 toasted multi grain English muffin 30g avocado 1 small tomato 1 medium size fruit	2 round crumpets 1 tsp Flora Light margarine 1 tsp honey	2 Weet-bix ¾ cup skim milk 1 medium size fruit	¾ cup All Bran cereal ¾ cup skim milk 1 cup canned peaches (no added sugar) drained
1 serve Meatball & Vegetable Soup BOOK 5 2 slices 9 grain bread 1 tsp Flora Light margarine 1 x 125g orange	1 50g multi grain bread roll 1 slice Bega Super Slim cheese 1 tsp Flora Light margarine 1½ cups salad 1 medium size fruit	1 lavash bread 30g 25% reduced fat tasty cheese 1½ cups salad 30g avocado 1 tbsp 97% ff mayonnaise 1 tub Diet Chocolate Mousse (Nestle)	1 50g multi grain bread roll 30g 97% ff ham 1 slice Bega Super Slim cheese 1½ cups salad 1 tsp 97% ff mayonnaise 1 medium size fruit
1 serve Chicken Pesto Pasta BOOK 5 *p 38* 2 cups vegetables or salad	1 serve Potato Lasagne *p 48* BOOK 5 2 cups vegetables or salad ¾ cup canned peaches (no sugar added) drained	1 Lean Cuisine Soy Beef with Wholemeal Noodles 2 cups vegetables or salad 1 medium size fruit	1 serve Chicken Enchilada BOOK 5 2 cups salad *p 37* 20g raw almonds
1 cup skim milk 1 x 200g diet fruit yoghurt 1 Uncle Toby's Crunchy Apricot Muesli Bar	1 cup skim milk 1 medium size fruit 1 All Bran baked bar	1 cup skim milk 1 medium size fruit 2 Ryvita crispbreads 1 tsp Flora Light margarine 2 tsps jam	¾ cup skim milk 1 x 200g diet fruit yoghurt 1 serve Apricot and Walnut Loaf BOOK 5
BREAKFAST - 30g more avocado SNACK - 1 x 44.5g Lite Mars Bar	SNACKS - 1 chocolate Paddle Pop, 25g raw almonds	BREAKFAST - 1 extra Weet-bix, ¼ cup more skim milk. LUNCH - 30g more avocado SNACK - 1 x 20g snack size potato chips	BREAKFAST - 1 slice 9 grain bread, 1 tsp Flora Light margarine, 1 tsp jam 15g more almonds

Day 25	Day 26	Day 27	Day 28
2 slices 9 grain toast 2 tsp peanut butter 1 medium size fruit	½ cup All Bran cereal ½ cup skim milk 1 medium size fruit	¾ cup cooked (30g raw) rolled oats made with water ½ cup skim milk 1 medium size fruit	1 slice 9 grain bread toast ½ cup canned spaghetti in tomato & cheese sauce 1 medium size fruit
1 50g multi grain bread roll 1 boiled egg 1 cup salad 1 tsp 97% ff mayonnaise 1 x 200g diet fruit yoghurt	1 Smoked Salmon Sandwich BOOK 5 *p 53* 1 cup salad 1 x 200g diet fruit yoghurt 1 medium size fruit	4 Ryvita crispbreads 30g 25% reduced fat tasty cheese 1½ cups salad 1 Weight Watchers Fruit Duo Cereal Bar 1 medium size fruit	4 Ryvita crispbreads 90g low fat cottage cheese 30g 97% ff ham 2 cups salad 2 tsps Flora Light margarine
1 Healthy Pastie BOOK 5 *p 13* 2 cups vegetables ¼ cup low joule gravy (Gravox)	125g raw lean rump steak (grill or BBQ) 1 serve Cajun Rice Salad BOOK 5 *p 26* 1 cup salad 2 slices Cheesy Pesto Bread BOOK 5 *p 16*	125g raw salmon fillet (cook with cooking spray in non stick frypan) *p 96* 1 serve Italian Potatoes BOOK 5 2 cups vegetables or salad 50g Peters Light n Creamy ice-cream	1 serve Lamb Kebabs BOOK 5 ¾ cup cooked Basmati rice 2 cups salad *p 47*
1 cup skim milk 250g fresh strawberries 1 Uncle Toby's Crunchy Apricot Muesli Bar	1 cup skim milk 250g fresh strawberries 1 serve Mango Passionfruit Cheesecake BOOK 5	1 cup skim milk 1 English multi grain muffin 2 tsps Flora Light margarine 1 tsp Vegemite 1 x 200g diet fruit yoghurt	1 cup skim milk 125g fresh kiwi fruit 1 serve Mango Passionfruit Cheesecake BOOK 5
SNACK - 50g Red Rock Deli chips	DINNER - 25g more raw lean rump steak & 1 extra slice Cheesy Pesto Bread. SNACK - 1 x 12g milk chocolate Freddo, 1 medium size fruit	DINNER - ½ serve more of Italian Potatoes SNACK - 30g dry roasted cashews (unsalted)	DINNER - ½ serve more Lamb Kebabs SNACK - 1 x 20g snack size potato chips

Dietitian's Tips

Written by Lisa Cochrane

B Sc. Grad Dip Diet.
MPH APD

Senior Dietitian
Diabetes Australia -
Victoria

Dietitian's Tip:
Look for these notes throughout the book for my tips & advice to assist people with diabetes.
Lisa Cochrane

Annette's recipe books stand out from the crowd and I believe that this, her fifth book, is the best one yet. Delicious tasting meals and snacks, loads of options within the meals and complete nutrition panels for every recipe are a few of the highlights of Annette's book. These are essential factors behind a good book but what makes this a great book is Annette's commitment to providing the healthiest food choices available through taking into consideration the latest health research.

Annette's recipes are suitable for anyone interested in having a long and healthy life. Through incorporating these recipes into your eating plan you may reduce your risk of developing specific types of cancers including breast and prostrate cancer and chronic diseases such as heart disease and type 2 diabetes. The recipes are also ideal for people who are working towards weight loss or those who are aiming to better manage their diabetes.

Are you on track to develop heart disease or type 2 diabetes?

With weight gain your body's fat cells, particularly around your waist, make it more difficult for insulin to move the glucose (sugar) out of your blood and into the body cells. Your body is also becoming insulin resistant.

For many people, as the pancreas gets more overworked it finally can no longer produce enough insulin to move the glucose from the blood stream. This is when diabetes is diagnosed.

Up to 90% of all people with type 2 diabetes are overweight or obese. Once diagnosed with type 2 diabetes you have it for life. It can be managed, and managed well through having a healthy lifestyle. You may also require medications such as oral hypoglycaemic or insulin, as well continuing to have a healthy lifestyle.

Break the cycle and reduce your risk of developing diabetes and heart disease.

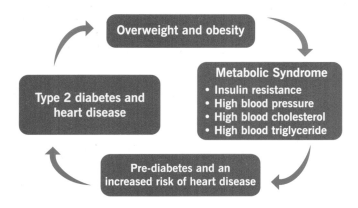

Overweight and obesity

Metabolic Syndrome
- Insulin resistance
- High blood pressure
- High blood cholesterol
- High blood triglyceride

Type 2 diabetes and heart disease

Pre-diabetes and an increased risk of heart disease

The good news is that weight loss can break the type 2 diabetes and heart disease cycle.

TRY ANNETTE'S 28-DAY MENU PLAN

Forget dieting. It does not work in the long run. What you need is a healthy eating plan. A great start would be trying Annette's 28-day menu plan that incorporates all of the food recommendations of the Dietary Guidelines for Australian Adults. Use this as a guide and then create your own menu plan.

CHOOSE RECIPES FROM THIS BOOK

Annette has spent considerable time to ensure that the recipes are low in total fat and saturated fat, making them ideal for managing heart disease. In addition, many of the recipes are high in fibre so your body feels fuller for longer than low fibre meals, helping with weight loss. Annette has also included many recipes that are low in sodium (salt) to help with controlling blood pressure and heart disease.

PORTION SIZES

Have you noticed how our meals are getting bigger? If you eat more food, even if it is healthy you will not lose weight, in fact you may even increase your weight. Annette's recipes are designed to provide a suitable amount of kilojoules for most people.

I ALREADY HAVE TYPE 2 DIABETES - WHAT CAN I DO?

HAVE THREE MEALS A DAY CONTAINING SOME CARBOHYDRATE FOODS

The total amount of carbohydrate that you eat has a greater impact on your blood glucose level than any other nutrient. This is because carbohydrates, which include sugars, are metabolised (broken down) in the body to glucose. Insulin takes the glucose from the blood and moves it into the body cells. For this reason it is advised that you have regular meals and include a moderate amount of carbohydrate in each meal and snack. If you have irregular meals of different carbohydrate amounts your blood glucose level will not be well controlled. The amount of carbohydrate in Annette's recipes is moderate.

INCLUDE LOW GLYCAEMIC INDEX FOODS IN YOUR EATING PLAN

The glycaemic index (GI) is a ranking of carbohydrate food according to its effect on blood glucose levels after eating. Foods with a low GI (less than 55), cause a slower increase in blood glucose over a longer time frame and are better choices than high GI foods (over 70) that cause a faster increase in blood glucose level. However, it is important to remember that foods with a low GI still need to be limited. If the total amount of carbohydrate is too high your blood glucose levels will be high even if the GI of the recipe is low.

THIS COOKBOOK HAS BEEN ENDORSED BY DIABETES AUSTRALIA.

Diabetes Australia is happy to assist with any questions or concerns you may have. Ring on their toll free number
1300 136588

DIABETES AUSTRALIA

THE SECRET TO WEIGHT LOSS SUCCESS

Do you want to lose weight, get healthy and live a longer and happier life? Don't we all! Most western countries have more overweight people than ever before in history. This is a real concern and if something isn't done soon we will have a world filled with people plagued with illness, such as Type 2 diabetes, heart disease, high cholesterol and cancer. Obese people also, have a shorter life span. My mission in life is to help change this. Apart from the few who suffer genetic or medical problems that cause weight gain, I believe there are four major factors that cause someone to become overweight.

WHY SOME PEOPLE ARE OVERWEIGHT

1. OVEREATING - Our dinner plates have gotten bigger and so have our serves. Children are eating meals the size of an adult's portion and adults are also eating way too much food. Do you eat just to eat? Do you eat to feed an emotion, or because you are bored or lonely? If you say yes to any of these then you need to make some serious changes. If you are overweight, then I guarantee you are overeating.

SOLUTION - Eat healthy food in moderate amounts. Remember that by following a healthy diet and exercising regularly, you will succeed. The perfect dinner plate should be half vegetables or salad, a quarter protein and a quarter carbohydrates. Take a look at my 28-day menu plan in this book, as this will show you how much you should be eating for healthy weight loss. If you want additional menu planning support, why not also consider my SYMPLY TOO GOOD TO BE TRUE CD-Rom Menu Planner. I remember when I first started to lose weight and I saw what 90g of cooked chicken looked like on my dinner plate. I was horrified, but now I would find that a huge portion size. Overeating, even healthy food, can cause weight gain and is one of the biggest issues overweight people have. Cut your portion sizes down and you too will become smaller.

2. BAD FOOD CHOICES - We are a time-poor society so convenient, prepackaged food, is common place. Ask yourself - do you eat food to energise your body or do you make food choices solely based on enjoyment? Over-consuming junk food, and eating too many takeaways and convenience foods, which are normally high in saturated fats, sugar and sodium (salt), will lead to ill health and obesity. How much of the food you choose is good for you and how much of it is causing you to be overweight?

SOLUTION - Ask yourself before you eat anything: "is this food good for me or just good for my taste buds?" Eat a low saturated fat diet, choose good quality carbs and proteins, increase your fibre intake and drink lots of water. Keep salt and sugar to a minimum and restrict how much alcohol and caffeine you have. Another good question to ask yourself is: "is this food going to give me energy and vitality or is it going to slow me down and cause weight gain?" You are in control of what you put in your mouth so only eat nutritious food. With all my fabulous recipes you have no excuse.

3. LACK OF PHYSICAL ACTIVITY - In today's society we are living fast and stressful lives, with little time to spend on exercising, but there is one thing that must be a priority and that is your health. Sitting for hours at a computer or television, or playing computer games has created couch crunchers. Our bodies are designed to move, so move it! We drive everywhere, have machines to do so much for us and never have the time to exercise but if we don't incorporate exercise into our week then we just don't move enough. This in turn leads to weight gain and ill health.

SOLUTION - Join a gym, get a dog and go walking, or if you don't want to go out to exercise then hire some exercise equipment, do exercise tapes or put some music on and dance around your house. Do anything that will increase your heart rate. Get out your basket ball, hockey stick or what ever you used to enjoy doing when you were young and join a team. My favourite ways to exercise are water aerobics, walking my dogs, working with my trainer Paul and doing weights at home. I also love squash. Get off your couch and get your heart rate up. Exercising will help you to have good muscle tone, fitness and energy, and will also assist in weight loss. Sounds good to me, so JUST DO IT.

4. LACK OF MOTIVATION - Unless you are committed and excited about losing weight and becoming a healthy person, it won't happen. You must change things if you don't want to stay as you are. The only reason people quit, is when motivation is lost or they allow excuses to stop them from continuing on their weight loss journey.

SOLUTION - I know from my own personal experience the challenge of losing weight, but I also know the rewards that await you so instead of thinking about what you are going to have to give up, think about what you will gain by sticking to a healthy regime. Focus on the positive and see yourself at goal weight trim, taut and terrific. We only have one life so make it the best life you can. When I was losing weight I would give myself small goals to achieve, then reward myself in some way whether it was to see a new release movie, buy a new top or some perfume. Do whatever works for you. When you are focused and committed it's amazing what you can achieve. Take responsibility for yourself and remember to keep your motivation alive no matter what and you will succeed. If getting motivated and staying that way is difficult for you, why not check out my SYMPLY TOO GOOD TO BE TRUE Motivational Audio CD. Each day for a whole month, you can hear how you can be empowered, motivated and in control of your weight loss, with motivational messages and positive quotes for the day. Above all never give up. Make a pact with yourself that you will not stop until you get to your desired weight, no matter how long it takes, how hard it is or how many excuses you make.

FINAL THOUGHTS

Don't let your emotions determine what you eat. If you eat when feeling upset, bored, frustrated, angry, happy or lonely then you must make some changes if you wish to lose weight. Be honest - how many times have you turned to chocolate or another comfort food to help ease whatever is upsetting or depressing you? You chomp your way through the packet only to feel much worse - not only are you still feeling depressed but now you also feel guilty.

Your attitude is the key to success. By loving yourself, never giving up on yourself and by changing bad habits you can create a lifestyle that is both healthy and happy. I am not asking you to do anything I haven't already done so step up and be your own best friend and above all value yourself. You have to be honest and responsible for your actions. Start now with a new belief system that puts you in control. Be empowered and let nothing stop you.

Testimonials

Many wonderful people have written letters, faxes and emails from all over the world. I feel blessed that so many people have taken the time out of their busy lives to write to me and I thank you all. I thought I would share some fantastic snippets from mail that I have received.

As a time-poor single parent and self confessed 'bad cook', I have been searching for years, for a way to spend less time in the kitchen and more time with my child and still manage to eat healthily. When I picked up number 3 of the Symply Too Good To Be True cook books, my world changed. My young son and I love the food and due to the extreme ease of the recipes, my time is spent doing things that I enjoy, not slaving over the stove. I now own the entire collection and can't wait for the next edition. I recommend these books to every parent on the planet. Believe me, your children will thank you.
Tina Shaw - Coolum QLD Publisher - The Single Parent Bible www.singleparentbible.com.au

I would like to say a very big thank you for your wonderful books. I have always been an emotional eater and 18 months ago I was diagnosed as having Impaired Glucose Tolerance and well on the way to developing full blown diabetes. After borrowing one of your books from a friend I went out and purchased all four copies at once, much to my husband's absolute horror. He has to admit now that they are the best things I have ever bought. Thanks to your books I now am "in control of my food" and no longer have food controlling me! I have lost 40kg, going from 100kg to 60kg and my husband has lost over 20kg. We both feel fantastic and have loads of energy. My sugar levels are normal now which is great. We exercise every day too and my books are "my bibles" - I am constantly poring over them and often refer to the testimonials and tips at the front of each book for inspiration! Thank you for sharing your wonderful recipes and for all your helpful tips. You have changed our lives for the better!
Pauline Lyon - Petrie QLD

Pauline before and after her weight loss of 40 kilos and Norman before and after his weight loss of 20 kilos.

My name is Chris I am a 62 year old male disabled pensioner. I had a weight problem. I was 136kg and getting heavier all the time. I was told about your four cookbooks and started using them. I have lost 38kg in 36 weeks without any exercise so I am very happy. I was borderline with a sugar problem but not any more. Thank you.
Christopher Smith - Ipswich QLD

Three years ago I was diagnosed with gastric reflux (aggravated by being 35kg overweight). Annette gave a talk to the TOWN Club (Take Off Weight Naturally) Western Region in Victoria. I attended and was absolutely inspired by her story and commonsense approach. I have now lost 17kg in six months and now know that I'm a healthy person and will never put on weight again.
Sr Rita Malavisi - Glenroy VIC

Karin before and after her weight loss of over 30 kilos.

Thank you so much for your cookbooks. I absolutely love them. I was introduced to them by my sister who uses them to help with her diabetes. I now use your cookbooks daily. I have lost over 30kg so far with your help and WW. I know I will get to my goal weight and be able to maintain it for the rest of my life.
Karin Griffiths - Leda WA

A friend told me about your books and am I glad she did. My doctor advised me to lose some weight and to give up junk food as I weighed 114 kilos and ate too much pizza and takeaway meals. Your recipes helped me to lose 46 kilos and I am now a happy and healthy 68 kilos. My favourite recipe is your lasagne in book one. Thank you Annette for your quick and easy recipes they really helped me lose the weight and to also keep it off. My husband Jason also thanks you.
Karen Guy - Currimundi QLD

We discovered your cookbooks while visiting my sister last year. My sister had been using your recipes and had lost 25 pounds and looked great. We even lost weight while we were there as they used your recipes all the time and we both came home five pounds lighter and had eaten really good food! We now have our own copies and so do my two daughters and sister who live in Canada. We all love them.
Jean Dodson - California, U.S.A.

Since buying your books I have lost 24.4kg in 6 months. I thank you for writing such great books; they have not only helped me but my whole family.
Rachelle Olsen - Corio VIC

When my mother-in-law showed me your books I was hooked instantly and bought all of your recipe books. After losing 40 kilos and still going I will never cook from anything else again. Even my family and friends love your food.
Lisa Davis - Korumburra VIC

I have never been much of a cook but with your easy recipe books I now am cooking up a storm and loving it. I have also managed to lose 12 kilos, which had been plaguing me for years, and have even lowered my cholesterol. Thank you for changing my life for the better.
Kasey Graham - Ryde NSW

Your recipes are so yummy even our young children are happy to eat the meals. It makes losing weight easy when we don't

have to cook separate meals. So far I have lost 27Kg and my husband has lost 17Kg. This is something we never thought we could achieve. We have never felt and looked so good. Thank you Annette.
Mark & Vicki Fraser - Lilydale VIC

Thank you for your wonderful books. I have all four since they were recommended to me by the dietitian after my heart by-pass operation. They have become my bibles and go everywhere with me, even when we travel in our caravan.
Tamara Genders - Mountain Creek QLD

Thanks Annette for giving us a simple and easy way to eating healthy. Both my wife and I turned the corner to a healthier lifestyle. I have said goodbye to 20kg in 20 weeks with the help of walking most days and your recipes. My doctor is more excited about me losing the kilos than I am, no more high blood pressure! My friends and family are amazed at our transformation.
Barrie Knott - Toowoomba QLD

I used your banana cake recipe for the Mt Larcom Show and one first prize in the cake section. This was the first time I had ever entered a cooking contest. Thanks very much for your help and great books.
Kate Kiernan - Gladstone QLD

Two and a half years ago I had a life and death situation while having a simple operation. My doctor said if I don't get the weight off I'll be dead in a year. I've tried all diets and spent thousands of dollars trying to look normal. I decided to have Gastric Lap Band surgery. With my surgery and the help of my special friend Annette, I achieved my goal of losing 72 kilos in 15 months and now I'm a healthy 72 kilos. Annette, you and your books inspired me all the way with your mouth watering low fat recipes and personal phone calls to keep me on track. The best was yet to come, when I won our T.O.W.N Club's highest weight loss award in 2005. You are an inspiration to all who are on their journey to a better lifestyle. Thank you for making me the person I am today.
Faye Wilson - Wallan VIC.

Faye before and after her weight loss of 72 kilos.

My cholesterol, thanks to medication and your recipes, has gone from 10 down to 4.4 in eight weeks. The lowest it has ever been and I am ecstatic.
Ann Menzies - Manoora QLD

My mum and I love eating your fabulous healthy food. My mum has lost 7 kilos and I want to be a chef or Aussie cook so thank you Annette for inspiring me to believe in myself and that I could go onto a diet and eat healthy!
Dane Harrison 11 years old - E. Bentleigh VIC

I would just like to thank you for giving me the inspiration to keep on keeping on. I have found you very inspiring. My dietitian suggested your cookbooks as I have diabetes, which at this stage is being controlled by diet and exercise. I have now lost 22 kilos and your recipes are yummy.
Debra Carringan - Tannum Sands Qld

Beaty before at size 20 and now a healthy size 8.

It was wonderful meeting you and getting my books signed in Townsville. I am a great believer in your books. I have type 2 diabetes and had to lose weight and was shown your books. I have now gone from size 20 to size 8. I have kept my weight down for the past few years and feel great. I had been taking blood pressure tablets for 13 years and now I don't have to, and my diabetes is under control. I hope this letter gives other readers encouragement.
Beaty Sterling - Oonoonba QLD

Thank you for your recipe books. I call them my bibles. My whole family loves the recipes, they are nice and easy for me as a busy wife and mother of four. I have managed to keep 28 kilos off since cooking with your books every day for the past few years.
Wendy Schwanda - Burnie TAS

I have tried various diets with short-term success, however the weight loss would always end up coming back. I am pleased to say I have just reached my goal weight thanks to the changes in lifestyle I achieved through better food choices, portion control and thanks to your excellent recipes. It has taken me 12 months to lose 45kg and I feel sure that I have reformed my bad eating habits so that I can keep the weight off for good. There is no doubt in my mind that your recipe books have improved my lifestyle in such a way to coin a familiar phrase, "Its SYMPLY TOO GOOD TO BE TRUE".
Peter Cathery - Mooroolbark VIC

I bought all your products six months ago. I have since gone from 108kg to 66kg, a loss of 42 kilos. Symply Too Good To Be True was the launch pad for my new lifestyle. I still use the recipes for myself and my children and we all benefit. Thank you for doing the hard yards and paving the way for me to walk and eat my way to fitness.
Felicity Jenner - Kallangur QLD

Your books are packed with recipes that are mindful of the fact that not everyone can buy exotic ingredients and don't want to spend four hours in the kitchen cooking dinner. I was asked how someone can lose weight eating the way I do. I say it is just "Symply Too Good To Be True". I have gone from a tight size 18 to a very loose size 14. I just couldn't believe how easy it was to lose weight using your recipes. I have to date lost 16kg.
Linda McGraw - Quaama NSW

Healthy Pasties

Healthy Pasties

SERVES: 4

FILLING

⅔ cup (100g) peeled potato small dice

½ cup swede small dice

½ cup carrot small dice

½ cup parsnip small dice

⅓ cup frozen peas

cooking spray

250g very lean beef mince

½ teaspoon crushed garlic (in jar)

⅓ cup onion small dice

2 teaspoons salt-reduced chicken-style stock powder

1 tablespoon no-added-salt tomato paste

PASTRY

2 tablespoons (30g) Flora Light® margarine

½ cup skim milk

1 egg white

¼ cup self-raising flour

1¼ cups plain flour

½ teaspoon salt-reduced vegetable stock powder

DIRECTIONS

Preheat oven 180°C fan forced.

To make filling: Microwave vegetables except onion on HIGH for 10 minutes or until just cooked through. In a large non-stick frypan that has been coated with cooking spray sauté mince, garlic and onion until cooked. Add stock powder, tomato paste and cooked vegetables and combine well. Leave to cool.

To make pastry: Melt margarine in microwave, add to milk and combine. Add egg white beating with a fork until blended. Sift both flours and stock powder into a medium size mixing bowl. Pour milk mixture into flour and combine.

To assemble pasties: Turn onto a floured surface and roll out pastry until thin enough to get four circle shapes (about 21cm in size). Use a small side plate or large saucer to cut circle. Place about ¾ cup of filling on one side of circle, wet edges with a pastry brush dipped into skim milk. Fold pastry over top of filling and press the edges together. Place pasties on a flat baking tray that has been generously coated with cooking spray then spray tops of pastry. Bake 25-30 minutes or until golden brown.

VARIATIONS: FOR A VEGETARIAN PASTIE OMIT MINCE AND REPLACE WITH ½ CUP CELERY SMALL DICE OR FOR A QUICKER PASTIE REPLACE PASTRY MIX WITH 4 SHEETS FILO PASTRY (ANTONIOU®).

FILO VARIATION DIRECTIONS

To assemble filo pasties: Using one filo sheet cut sheet into two long strips, spray pastry with cooking spray then place one sheet on top of the other. Place about ¾ cup of filling onto top corner of strip, fold mixture over to other side diagonally. Continue folding diagonally until you reach the end of the strip. Place onto a flat baking tray that has been coated with cooking spray and spray top of pastry. Repeat this method until 4 pasties are made. Bake 25-30 minutes or until golden brown.

Dietitian's Tip

Try the filo option for a quick, healthy meal low in fat and kilojoules making them ideal for those with heart disease or diabetes.

Nutritional Information ⓕ

PER SERVE		BEEF	VEGETARIAN	BEEF FILO	VEG FILO
FAT	TOTAL	8.8g	4.5g	5.0g	0.7g
	SATURATED	2.7g	0.9g	1.9g	0.1g
FIBRE		4.7g	5.0g	2.7g	3.0g
PROTEIN		22.6g	10.0g	17.1g	4.5g
CARBS		47.3g	47.7g	19.9g	20.2g
SUGAR		5.1g	5.3g	3.6g	3.8g
SODIUM		180mg	155mg	190mg	165mg
KILOJOULES		1516 (cals 361)	1149 (cals 274)	812 (cals 193)	445 (cals 106)
GI RATING		MEDIUM	MEDIUM	MEDIUM	MEDIUM

Creamy Chicken and Vegetable Soup

SERVES: 8

cooking spray
2 teaspoons crushed garlic (in jar)
400g skinless chicken breast small dice
1 large onion diced
1 cup carrot diced
1 cup frozen peas
1 cup frozen corn kernels
1 litre water
4 tablespoons salt-reduced chicken-style stock powder
½ teaspoon dried tarragon
½ cup (76g) raw macaroni pasta
2 cups skim milk
1 x 375ml can evaporated light milk
2 tablespoons fresh parsley chopped
pepper to taste

Dietitian's Tip
A creamy soup packed with protein, vitamins and minerals and still low in fat. Thanks Annette.

DIRECTIONS

In a boiler or stock pot that has been generously coated with cooking spray, sauté garlic and chicken for 1 minute. Add onion and carrots and cook 1 minute. Add peas and corn, cook 1 minute more. Add water, stock powder and tarragon, bring to boil. Add raw pasta stirring in well, bring to boil. Reduce to a medium boil for 20 minutes, stirring occasionally. Add skim milk, evaporated milk, parsley and pepper, stir in well. Once boiled serve.

Nutritional Information Ⓕ

PER SERVE

FAT	TOTAL	2.4g
	SATURATED	0.9g
FIBRE		3.3g
PROTEIN		18.8g
CARBS		19.9g
SUGAR		8.1g
SODIUM		112mg
KILOJOULES		743 (cals 177)
GI RATING		LOW

Swedish Pitti Panna

SERVES: 6

500g raw lean rump steak
1½ kilos potatoes
1 large onion
275g 97% fat-free hot dogs
cooking spray
6 whole eggs (optional)

Dietitian's Tip
Potatoes contain many vitamins & minerals however they have a high GI. To balance this have a low GI dessert such as a low fat yoghurt, slice of mango or an orange.

DIRECTIONS

Grill steak until cooked to your liking, cut into small dice and leave to one side. Peel and dice potatoes. Dice onion and hot dogs (try to keep dice size similar). In a large non-stick frypan that has been generously coated with cooking spray, sauté potatoes for 10 minutes or until nearly cooked. Occasionally spray potato with cooking spray so that the potato doesn't burn. Add onion to pan, cook 2 minutes. Add steak and hot dogs and toss together until combined and heated through. Divide mixture evenly over 6 dinner plates. Coat frypan generously with cooking spray and fry eggs. Place each egg on top of meat mixture and serve.

SUITABLE TO BE FROZEN MINUS EGG

ANNETTE'S TIP: This recipe is a great way to use up left over lean steak from BBQs.

Nutritional Information Ⓕ

PER SERVE		WITH EGG	WITHOUT EGG
FAT	TOTAL	10.5g	5.4g
	SATURATED	3.7g	2.1g
FIBRE		4.3g	4.3g
PROTEIN		36.4g	30.0g
CARBS		36.9g	36.7g
SUGAR		2.6g	2.5g
SODIUM		564mg	497mg
KILOJOULES		1720 (cals 410)	1423 (cals 339)
GI RATING		HIGH	HIGH

Meatball and Vegetable Soup

SERVES: 8

MEATBALLS

300g very lean beef mince

1 egg white

1 teaspoon tomato sauce

1 teaspoon BBQ sauce

SOUP

cooking spray

1 cup onion diced

1 cup carrot diced

1 cup turnip diced

1 cup parsnip diced

1 cup celery diced

1 cup swede diced

2 teaspoons crushed garlic (in jar)

2 tablespoons Worcestershire sauce

3 tablespoons soy sauce 43% low salt

3 tablespoons salt-reduced chicken-style stock powder

3 litres water

½ cup dried soup mix

2 teaspoons dried oregano leaves

¼ cup fresh parsley chopped

pepper to taste

DIRECTIONS

To make meatballs: In a small mixing bowl combine meatball ingredients and mix well. Roll into small meatballs, about 1 teaspoon of mixture for each meatball. Leave to one side.

To make soup: In a boiler or stock pot that has been generously coated with cooking spray, sauté all vegetables and garlic for 3 minutes. Add all remaining ingredients to pot except meatballs, parsley and pepper. Bring to boil, carefully drop meatballs into pot. Return to boil then reduce to medium boil for 30 minutes or until vegetables are cooked. Add parsley and pepper.

VARIATIONS: REPLACE BEEF MINCE WITH LEAN CHICKEN, PORK OR LAMB MINCE.

Dietitian's Tip
This is a great choice for people wanting tasty soup without the added sodium (salt). Suitable for those with high blood pressure.

Nutritional Information ⓕ

PER SERVE		BEEF	CHICKEN	PORK	LAMB
FAT	TOTAL	2.8g	3.2g	2.8g	2.8g
	SATURATED	1.2g	1.0g	1.0g	1.2g
FIBRE		3.3g	3.3g	3.3g	3.3g
PROTEIN		10.6g	10.1g	10.4g	10.6g
CARBS		8.6g	8.6g	8.6g	8.6g
SUGAR		4.9g	4.9g	4.9g	4.9g
SODIUM		306mg	311mg	306mg	309mg
KILOJOULES		430 (cals 102)	440 (cals 105)	430 (cals 102)	431 (cals 103)
GI RATING		TOO LOW IN CARBS TO SCORE A RATING			

Olive Bread

MAKES: 15 SLICES

⅓ cup seedless Spanish black olives sliced

3 tablespoons grated parmesan cheese

½ small salad onion chopped

½ teaspoon crushed garlic (in jar)

½ teaspoon salt-reduced vegetable stock powder

1 x 170g French bread stick

DIRECTIONS

Place all ingredients except bread stick into a small bowl. Use a Bamix® to process ingredients together until a smooth paste is achieved. Cut bread stick into 15 slices, spread an even amount of paste over the top of each slice. Place under griller until browned. Serve as a starter or to accompany a meal.

SUITABLE TO BE FROZEN BEFORE GRILLING

Dietitian's Tip

Eat this bread slowly and make the most of the fabulous flavours knowing that it is low in fat and kilojoules - just right for a healthy body.

Nutritional Information Ⓕ

PER SERVE		
FAT	TOTAL	1.0g
	SATURATED	0.3g
FIBRE		0.5g
PROTEIN		1.6g
CARBS		6.4g
SUGAR		0.6g
SODIUM		101mg
KILOJOULES		171 (cals 41)
GI RATING		TOO LOW IN CARBS TO SCORE A RATING

Cheesy Pesto Bread

MAKES: 15 SLICES

1 x 170g French bread stick

6 teaspoons traditional pesto (in jar)

⅓ cup 25% reduced-fat grated tasty cheese

DIRECTIONS

Cut bread stick into 15 slices. Spread a little pesto over top of each slice. Place bread onto a flat baking tray then sprinkle a little grated cheese over each slice of bread. Place under griller and cook until cheese has melted. Serve as a starter or to accompany a meal.

SUITABLE TO BE FROZEN BEFORE GRILLING

Dietitian's Tip

Through using reduced fat grated cheese sparingly in this recipe you'll get tasty bread without excessive total fat, saturated fat and kilojoules.

Nutritional Information Ⓕ

PER SERVE		
FAT	TOTAL	1.8g
	SATURATED	0.6g
FIBRE		0.5g
PROTEIN		2.0g
CARBS		6.0g
SUGAR		0.5g
SODIUM		103mg
KILOJOULES		204 (cals 49)
GI RATING		TOO LOW IN CARBS TO SCORE A RATING

Thai Beef Noodle Salad

SERVES: 4

DRESSING

¼ cup fresh lime juice

¼ cup water

½ teaspoon crushed garlic (in jar)

½ teaspoon crushed ginger (in jar)

2 teaspoons soy sauce 43% less salt

1 tablespoon Thai chilli stir fry paste

2 teaspoons lemongrass chopped (in jar)

1 tablespoon fresh coriander leaves chopped

1 tablespoon sugar

SALAD

4 cups gourmet lettuce

125g Lebanese cucumber sliced

20 cherry tomatoes cut in half

¾ cup capsicum sliced

1 carrot thinly sliced

15 snow peas thinly sliced on angle

⅓ cup shallots thinly sliced on angle

100g dried vermicelli noodles

400g raw lean rump steak

4 teaspoons Thai seasoning

cooking spray

DIRECTIONS

To make dressing: Place all dressing ingredients in a small mixing bowl and combine well.

To make salad: Divide salad ingredients equally over 4 dinner plates. To prepare noodles follow instructions on packet. Coat steak with Thai seasoning. In a non-stick frypan that has been generously coated with cooking spray, fry steak until cooked to your liking. Cut into thin strips and leave to one side. Place noodles on top of salad then put rump slices over top. Pour dressing over salad.

VARIATIONS: REPLACE STEAK WITH 400g LEAN LAMB LEG STEAKS, 400g SKINLESS CHICKEN BREASTS, 400g PEELED RAW PRAWNS OR 400g TOFU DICED.

Dietitian's Tip
The prawn variation is higher in sodium (salt) compared with the red meat, chicken and fish. Choose this option on special occasions or pick the other variations instead.

Nutritional Information

PER SERVE		RUMP	LAMB	CHICKEN	PRAWN
FAT	TOTAL	3.4g	3.0g	3.1g	1.4g
	SATURATED	1.2g	1.1g	0.7g	0.2g
FIBRE		3.5g	3.5g	3.5g	3.5g
PROTEIN		26.8g	26.2g	26.0g	23.9g
CARBS		19.3g	19.3g	19.3g	19.3g
SUGAR		8.5g	8.5g	8.5g	8.5g
SODIUM		235mg	249mg	240mg	540mg
KILOJOULES		915 (cals 218)	890 (cals 212)	890 (cals 212)	792 (cals 189)
GI RATING		LOW	LOW	LOW	LOW

Tacos

MAKES: 12 REGULAR SIZE TACOS

FILLING

1 x 420g can kidney beans

cooking spray

250g very lean beef mince

1 teaspoon crushed garlic (in jar)

½ cup onion finely diced

1 x 415g can no-added-salt crushed tomatoes

4 tablespoons no-added-salt tomato paste

1 teaspoon salt-reduced chicken-style stock powder

2 tablespoons reduced-salt taco seasoning

TACO

12 taco shells regular size

⅓ cup 25% reduced-fat grated tasty cheese

1½ cups fresh tomatoes small dice

3 cups lettuce finely shredded

ADD ON EXTRAS PER TACO

1 teaspoon extra-light sour cream (add 0.6g fat)

1 teaspoon avocado mashed (add 1.1g fat)

DIRECTIONS

To make filling: Drain and rinse kidney beans. In a non-stick frypan that has been generously coated with cooking spray, sauté mince and garlic until browned. Add onion and cook 2 minutes. Add canned tomatoes, tomato paste, stock powder and taco seasoning stirring well. Fold in kidney beans and simmer 3 minutes.

To cook taco shells: Follow cooking instructions on packet.

To assemble: In each taco shell spoon one twelfth of meat mixture, top with 1 teaspoon of cheese, about 2 tablespoons fresh tomato and ¼ cup lettuce, repeat this process for each taco shell.

VARIATIONS: REPLACE BEEF MINCE WITH LEAN CHICKEN MINCE OR FOR A VEGETARIAN VERSION REPLACE MINCE WITH 1 x 420g CAN 4 BEAN MIX DRAINED AND WASHED & REPLACE CHICKEN STOCK POWDER WITH SALT-REDUCED VEGETABLE STOCK POWDER.

TACO FILLING SUITABLE TO BE FROZEN

Dietitian's Tip

These tacos are packed with vitamins, minerals and antioxidants. Family members will enjoy being involved in assembling their own meals. A great introduction for children to the art of healthy cooking.

Nutritional Information Ⓕ

PER SERVE		BEEF	CHICKEN	VEGETARIAN
FAT	TOTAL	5.5g	5.7g	4.2g
	SATURATED	1.6g	1.5g	1.0g
FIBRE		3.3g	3.3g	5.1g
PROTEIN		8.4g	8.1g	5.8g
CARBS		13.0g	13.0g	16.5g
SUGAR		3.1g	3.1g	3.6g
SODIUM		244mg	247mg	285mg
KILOJOULES		570 (cals 136)	575 (cals 137)	552 (cals 131)
GI RATING		MEDIUM	MEDIUM	MEDIUM

Dahl Soup

SERVES: 6

¾ cup brown lentils

1 cup yellow split peas

cooking spray

2 medium onions diced

2 teaspoons crushed garlic (in jar)

1 teaspoon garam masala

2 teaspoons turmeric

1 tablespoon mustard seeds

1 tablespoon cumin

2 teaspoons dried coriander

1 teaspoon ground ginger

4 tablespoons salt-reduced vegetable stock powder

2 tablespoons no-added-salt tomato paste

2½ litres water

1 x 375ml can evaporated light milk

DIRECTIONS

Soak lentils and peas in water overnight as instructed on packet. Drain and rinse well. In a boiler or stock pot that has been generously coated with cooking spray, sauté onion and garlic for 2 minutes. Add all the spices and combine well, cook 1 minute. Add lentils and peas to pot with stock powder, tomato paste and water. Stir well and bring to boil. Reduce to a slow boil for 60 minutes. Add evaporated milk and bring back to boil. Using either a food processor or Bamix® blend ingredients until smooth in texture.

Nutritional Information

PER SERVE

FAT	TOTAL	1.9g
	SATURATED	0.6g
FIBRE		5.6g
PROTEIN		15.0g
CARBS		27.5g
SUGAR		7.9g
SODIUM		66mg
KILOJOULES		766 (cals 182)
GI RATING		LOW

Annie's Fruit Punch

MAKES: 20 CUPS

1 x 850ml pear and peach juice

1 x 850ml mango juice

1 x 1.25 litres low-joule lemonade

1 x 1.25 litres low-joule ginger ale

½ x 400g can fruit salad in natural juice

ice cubes (optional)

DIRECTIONS

Have all fruit juices and soft drinks well chilled. Pour all ingredients into a punch bowl. Add a few ice cubes if you wish. Stir punch before serving.

VARIATIONS: REPLACE WITH JUICE OF YOUR CHOICE OR REPLACE FRUIT SALAD WITH CANNED CRUSHED PINEAPPLE OR ½ A PUNNET DICED FRESH STRAWBERRIES OR 1 CUP DICED WATERMELON.

Nutritional Information

PER SERVE

FAT	TOTAL	0.1g
	SATURATED	0g
FIBRE		0.1g
PROTEIN		0.4g
CARBS		11.7g
SUGAR		11.2g
SODIUM		18mg
KILOJOULES		207 (cals 49)
GI RATING		MEDIUM

Chinese Omelette

SERVES: 2

3 egg whites

2 whole eggs

1 teaspoon salt-reduced chicken-style stock powder

cooking spray

¼ cup shallots sliced

½ cup mushrooms sliced

¼ cup frozen peas

1½ cups bean shoots

SAUCE

1 teaspoon cornflour

2 teaspoons oyster sauce

⅓ cup water

Dietitian's Tip

The Dietary Guidelines for Australians recommend eating at least 5 serves of vegetables a day. This omelette provides an ideal way to include vegetable in a healthy eating plan for people with diabetes or heart disease.

DIRECTIONS

To make omelette: Using a whisk, beat egg whites, whole eggs and stock powder together in a bowl. In a medium size non-stick frypan that has been generously coated with cooking spray, sauté shallots, mushrooms, peas and bean shoots for 2 minutes. Spread vegetables out evenly in the pan, pour egg mix over the top. Cook until egg mixture has browned on bottom (it should be still runny on top), don't have the heat too hot or it will burn bottom of omelette. Place frypan under a heated griller until omelette is cooked on top. Cut in half and carefully lift omelette onto plates.

To make sauce: Combine cornflour and oyster sauce with water then pour into pan, stir well until boiled. Pour sauce over omelette.

VARIATIONS: FOR A CHICKEN OMELETTE - IN A SMALL NON-STICK FRYPAN THAT HAS BEEN GENEROUSLY COATED WITH COOKING SPRAY, FRY 80g RAW SKINLESS CHICKEN BREAST UNTIL COOKED, SHRED; OR FOR A HAM OMELETTE ADD 40g LEAN HAM, SLICED; OR FOR A PRAWN OMELETTE ADD 60g COOKED PEELED PRAWNS, CUT IN HALF. ADD TO VEGETABLE MIX.

Nutritional Information

PER SERVE		PLAIN	CHICKEN	HAM	PRAWN
FAT	TOTAL	5.4g	7.6g	6.0g	5.7g
	SATURATED	1.6g	2.2g	1.8g	1.7g
FIBRE		4.0g	4.0g	4.0g	4.0g
PROTEIN		16.3g	24.8g	19.6g	22.7g
CARBS		7.4g	7.4g	7.4g	7.4g
SUGAR		2.9g	2.9g	2.9g	2.9g
SODIUM		400mg	424mg	512mg	522mg
KILOJOULES		601(cals 143)	828(cals 197)	687(cals 164)	725(cals 173)
GI RATING		TOO LOW IN CARBS TO SCORE A RATING			

Smoked Salmon Potato Cakes

SERVES: 6

600g potatoes peeled and diced

125g Light Philadelphia® cream cheese

1 cup dried breadcrumbs

1 tablespoon fresh lemon juice

1 teaspoon crushed garlic (in jar)

200g sliced smoked salmon diced

20 capers chopped

¼ cup shallots sliced

2 teaspoons salt-reduced vegetable stock powder

cooking spray

DIRECTIONS

Microwave potatoes on HIGH in a little water until cooked (about 10 minutes), drain well. In a large mixing bowl mash potato, add cream cheese and breadcrumbs. Place all remaining ingredients into bowl and combine well (you may need to use your hands). Shape into 12 round patties. In a large non-stick frypan that has been generously coated with cooking spray, fry potato cakes for 3 minutes or until browned. Coat tops of potato cakes with cooking spray, turn and cook a further 3 minutes or until browned on both sides.

Dietitian's Tip

Salmon is a great source of omega 3 fats making it an excellent choice for people with diabetes or anyone interested in good health.

Nutritional Information (F)

PER SERVE

FAT	TOTAL	9.0g
	SATURATED	1.2g
FIBRE		1.8g
PROTEIN		5.7g
CARBS		18.1g
SUGAR		1.8g
SODIUM		474mg
KILOJOULES		851 (cals 203)
GI RATING		HIGH

Vegetables and Salads

Top left: Grilled Vegetable Couscous Salad, Right: Carrot & Corn Salad, Front: Bean Salad.

Grilled Vegetable Couscous Salad

SERVES: 8 AS A SIDE DISH

SALAD: 1 medium size red capsicum
cooking spray
1 cup sweet potato
2 small zucchinis
2 small Lebanese eggplants
1¼ cups raw couscous
1¼ cups boiling water
1 tablespoon (15g) Flora Light® margarine
1 small salad onion
⅓ cup (60g) low-fat sun-dried tomatoes
3 tablespoons fresh parsley chopped
pepper to taste

DRESSING: ⅓ cup fat-free French dressing
2 teaspoons Dijon mustard (in jar)
½ teaspoon crushed ginger (in jar)
1 teaspoon oyster sauce

> **Dietitian's Tip**
> This salad provides a great way to boost your vegetable intake. Aim for 5 serves of vegetables a day.

DIRECTIONS

To prepare salad: Cut capsicum in half, core and de-seed. Place skin side up on a baking tray that has been coated with cooking spray, spray tops of capsicum and place under hot griller until browned, turning once. Leave to cool then remove skin from capsicum, leave to one side.

Dice sweet potato into medium size pieces. Slice zucchini and eggplant into 1cm slices. Place prepared vegetables onto a flat baking tray that has been generously coated with cooking spray. Spray tops of vegetables and place under hot griller until browned, turning once. Leave to one side.

To make couscous: Place couscous in a medium size saucepan (that has a lid), add boiling water and combine. Cook covered on low heat for 3 minutes. Using a fork, fluff couscous then fold in margarine.

Cut onion in quarters then slice thinly. Cut sun-dried tomatoes in half. Place all salad ingredients into a large mixing bowl, gently fold together.

To make dressing: Place all ingredients into a small mixing bowl and blend using a whisk. Pour dressing over salad and fold together.

Carrot and Corn Salad

SERVES: 8 AS A SIDE DISH

½ cup frozen corn kernels
¼ cup (30g) pine nuts
2 tablespoons sesame seeds
500g carrots grated
¼ cup corn relish (in jar)
⅓ cup salad onion finely diced
¼ cup currants
pepper to taste

> **Dietitian's Tip**
> Carrots contain lots of beta-carotene also called vitamin A. Carotenoid containing foods may be protective against some cancers such as lung and prostate.

DIRECTIONS

Microwave corn with a little water on HIGH for 2 minutes. Drain well then leave to cool. Place pine nuts and sesame seeds on a sheet of aluminum foil, place under griller and toast until browned. Be careful as they burn quickly. Leave to one side. Place all ingredients into a medium size mixing bowl, fold together until well combined.

Bean Salad

SERVES: 10 AS A SIDE DISH

DRESSING
½ cup Italian 100% fat-free salad dressing
½ teaspoon crushed garlic (in jar)
1 tablespoon BBQ sauce
2 teaspoons Thai chilli stir fry paste

SALAD
1 x 400g can kidney beans
1 x 400g can cannellini beans
1 x 400g can borlotti beans
1 cup fresh green beans sliced
1 cup mung beans
1 small salad onion diced
½ cup celery sliced
½ cup capsicum diced
1 cup fresh tomatoes diced
pepper to taste

> **Dietitian's Tip**
> Legumes such as kidney, cannellini and borlotti beans are an ideal source of protein and fibre. They have a low GI making the meal perfect for those aiming to lose weight, control diabetes or manage heart disease.

DIRECTIONS

In a small bowl combine all salad dressing ingredients. Drain and wash all canned beans. Place all ingredients including dressing into a large mixing bowl and fold together until well combined.

PER SERVE		Grilled Veg & Couscous	Carrot & Corn	Bean
FAT	TOTAL	2.2g	3.7g	0.6g
	SATURATED	0.3g	0.3g	0.1g
FIBRE		2.0g	2.9g	5.5g
PROTEIN		5.6g	1.9g	5.2g
CARBS		26.8g	11.1g	12.7g
SUGAR		5.6g	8.4g	3.4g
SODIUM		321mg	65mg	314mg
KILOJOULES		623 (cals 150)	354 (cals 84)	325 (cals 77)
GI RATING		MEDIUM	LOW	LOW

Nutritional Information for all 3 Salads

Mushroom and Bacon Salad

SERVES: 6

750g medium size mushrooms

1 bunch fresh asparagus

cooking spray

1 teaspoon crushed garlic (in jar)

100g bacon short cuts diced

1 cup capsicum diced

½ cup shallots sliced

½ cup low-fat sun-dried tomatoes

2 tablespoons fresh parsley chopped

DRESSING

⅓ cup Italian 100% fat-free dressing

½ teaspoon crushed garlic (in jar)

1 teaspoon soy sauce 43% less salt

2 teaspoons Dijon mustard

DIRECTIONS

Cut mushrooms into quarters. Cut 3cm off ends of asparagus spears and discard ends, cut spears into 2cm pieces. Generously coat a large non-stick frypan (that has a lid) with cooking spray and sauté garlic and bacon until browned. Add asparagus and capsicum and toss together for 2 minutes. Stir mushrooms through mixture then place lid on and cook 2 minutes or until mushrooms are just cooked and still firm. Add shallots, sun-dried tomatoes and parsley and fold through. Pour into a large bowl, draining any liquid, leave to cool.

To make dressing: In a small mixing bowl whisk all ingredients together. Once salad has cooled, drain any extra liquid that has settled at the bottom before pouring dressing over salad. Combine well. Refrigerate.

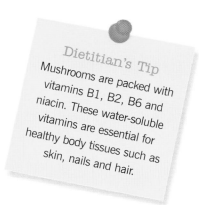

Dietitian's Tip

Mushrooms are packed with vitamins B1, B2, B6 and niacin. These water-soluble vitamins are essential for healthy body tissues such as skin, nails and hair.

Nutritional Information

PER SERVE

FAT	TOTAL	3.0g
	SATURATED	0.8g
FIBRE		2.3g
PROTEIN		5.6g
CARBS		3.6g
SUGAR		2.5g
SODIUM		353mg
KILOJOULES		266 (cals 63)
GI RATING		TOO LOW IN CARBS TO SCORE A RATING

Roasted Pumpkin and Spinach Pie

SERVES: 6

cooking spray
3 cups (300g) raw pumpkin cut in 1cm dice

PASTRY

¾ cup plain flour
¼ cup self-raising flour
2 tablespoons (30g) Flora Light® margarine
1½ tablespoons skim milk
1 egg white

FILLING

1 teaspoon crushed garlic (in jar)
1 onion diced
1 bunch English spinach roughly chopped
2 whole eggs
2 egg whites
1½ cups skim milk
2 tablespoons grated parmesan cheese
2 teaspoons salt-reduced vegetable stock powder
½ cup 25% reduced-fat grated tasty cheese

DIRECTIONS

Preheat oven 180°C fan forced.

On a flat baking tray that has been generously coated with cooking spray, place diced pumpkin, coat with cooking spray. Bake 25 minutes or until browned.

To make pastry: In a medium size mixing bowl combine flours together. Melt margarine then add to milk. Beat egg white into milk using a fork, pour into flour. Fold ingredients, if needed use your hands to help combine pastry. Place on a well floured surface and roll out to fit a 23cm pie plate that has been coated with cooking spray.

To make filling: Coat a non-stick frypan with cooking spray and sauté garlic and onion for 1 minute. Add spinach and toss until spinach has softened. In a large mixing bowl beat whole eggs and whites using an electric beater for 1 minute. Add milk, parmesan, stock powder, beat well. Spoon spinach over pastry base then sprinkle diced pumpkin over top. Pour egg mix over vegetables, sprinkle with grated cheese. Bake 40 minutes or until cooked in centre and browned. Serve hot or cold.

Dietitian's Tip

Generally pies are high in fat and particularly saturated fat. Annette has cleverly developed a pastry lower in all fats and suitable for people with diabetes.

Nutritional Information ⓕ

PER SERVE

FAT	TOTAL	8.0g
	SATURATED	3.3g
FIBRE		3.2g
PROTEIN		15.2g
CARBS		24.5g
SUGAR		6.7g
SODIUM		263mg
KILOJOULES		969 (cals 231)
GI RATING		MEDIUM

Cajun Rice Salad

SERVES: 8 AS A SIDE DISH

- 1 teaspoon turmeric
- 2 teaspoons salt-reduced vegetable stock powder
- 1½ cups raw Basmati rice
- ½ cup carrots finely diced
- ½ cup frozen peas
- ½ cup frozen corn kernels
- ½ cup frozen cut green beans
- ½ cup Spanish onion sliced
- 2 teaspoons Cajun seasoning
- ½ cup 97% fat-free mayonnaise
- pepper

Dietitian's Tip
A high carbohydrate salad loaded with vitamins and minerals. For a complete meal select a low carbohydrate meat or fish dish.

DIRECTIONS

Bring a large saucepan one third filled with water to boil. Once boiling, add turmeric, stock powder and rice, stir well. Reduce to slow boil. After 5 minutes add carrots, peas, corn and beans. Add extra water if needed and stir occasionally to avoid rice sticking to base of saucepan. Once rice is cooked, turn out into a colander and rinse well. In a large mixing bowl add rice and onion. Combine Cajun seasoning and mayonnaise together, add to bowl and mix in well. Pepper to taste.

VARIATION: OMIT TURMERIC FOR A WHITE RICE SALAD.

Italian Potatoes

SERVES: 6 AS A SIDE DISH

- 1 kilo potatoes
- 3 tablespoons grated parmesan cheese
- 1 tablespoon dried basil
- 1 teaspoon crushed garlic (in jar)
- cooking spray

DIRECTIONS

Preheat oven 230°C fan forced. Peel potatoes, cut into slices. Microwave with a little water on HIGH for 5 minutes. Drain well. Place potato slices in a large freezer bag with parmesan cheese, basil and garlic. Tie top then shake bag so ingredients coat potato. On a flat baking tray that has been generously coated with cooking spray, place slices evenly onto tray then coat tops of potato with cooking spray. Bake 30-35 minutes or until golden brown.

VARIATION: REPLACE POTATO WITH SWEET POTATO.

Dietitian's Tip
Annette has developed spicy low-fat chips that can be included in the eating plan of people with diabetes and heart disease.

Nutritional Information ⓕ

PER SERVE

FAT	TOTAL	0.8g
	SATURATED	0.2g
FIBRE		2.4g
PROTEIN		3.9g
CARBS		39.6g
SUGAR		6.2g
SODIUM		195mg
KILOJOULES		767 (cals 183)
GI RATING		MEDIUM

Nutritional Information ⓕ

PER SERVE

FAT	TOTAL	1.3g
	SATURATED	0.7g
FIBRE		2.3g
PROTEIN		4.7g
CARBS		18.5g
SUGAR		0.7g
SODIUM		53mg
KILOJOULES		446 (cals 106)
GI RATING		HIGH

Vegetarian Pie

SERVES: 6

cooking spray
1 teaspoon crushed garlic (in jar)
1 medium onion small dice
1 cup gold sweet potato small dice
1 cup celery small dice
1½ cups carrot small dice
1 cup frozen peas
1 x 415g can savoury lentils (Sanitarium®)
4 tablespoons no-added-salt tomato paste
1 teaspoon Worcestershire sauce
2 teaspoons salt-reduced vegetable
stock powder
3 tablespoons Gravox® Lite Supreme
1 cup water
pepper

PASTRY: 1 cup wholemeal self-raising flour
1 cup self-raising flour
3 tablespoons (45g) Flora Light® margarine melted
½ cup skim milk
1 egg white

DIRECTIONS

Preheat oven 180°C fan forced. In a large non-stick frypan that has been generously coated with cooking spray, sauté garlic, onion, sweet potato, celery and carrot for 5 minutes stirring occasionally. Add peas, lentils, tomato paste, Worcestershire sauce, stock powder and combine. Blend Gravox with water then add to pan and stir well. Pepper to taste.

To make pastry: In a medium size mixing bowl sift both flours together. Add melted margarine to milk, beat in egg white with a fork then pour into flour. Gently fold together, if needed use your hands to combine the pastry. Divide in half. On a well floured surface roll out one half to fit a 23cm pie dish that has been coated with cooking spray. Roll up pastry using a rolling pin, lift into pie plate. Place pie filling evenly on top of pastry. Brush a little skim milk around edges. Roll out remaining pastry and place on top. Pinch edges together. Brush with a little skim milk then cut a small slit in top of pie. Bake 30-35 minutes.

VARIATION: FOR A QUICKER PIE REPLACE PASTRY WITH 7 SHEETS FILO PASTRY. CUT EACH SHEET IN HALF (8 FOR BASE, 6 FOR TOP). LAYER PIE DISH WITH 8 CUT SHEETS OF PASTRY IN A ROTATING FASHION, SPRAYING WITH COOKING SPRAY BETWEEN EACH LAYER. SPOON MIXTURE EVENLY ON TOP THEN COVER WITH REMAINING 6 SHEETS IN A ROTATING FASHION. CRINKLE EDGES TOGETHER THEN SPRAY WITH COOKING SPRAY. CUT A SMALL SLIT IN TOP OF PASTRY, BAKE 30-35 MINUTES. SERVE IMMEDIATELY AS THE PASTRY WILL SOFTEN WHEN LEFT. TO CRISP AGAIN EITHER PLACE BACK IN OVEN OR UNDER GRILLER.

Dietitian's Tip

Lentils are a great source of soluble fibre. Soluble fibre helps to stabilise blood glucose levels in people with diabetes and may help to lower LDL (bad) cholesterol and therefore decrease the risk of heart disease.

Nutritional Information (F)

PER SERVE		PASTRY	FILO
FAT	TOTAL	4.9g	0.9g
	SATURATED	0.9g	0.1g
FIBRE		8.7g	5.0g
PROTEIN		12.8g	8.4g
CARBS		47.8g	30.6g
SUGAR		7.3g	6.2g
SODIUM		512mg	449mg
KILOJOULES		1228 (cals 292)	716 (cals 170)
GI RATING		MEDIUM	LOW

Vegetable Crumble

SERVES: 4 AS A SIDE DISH

FILLING

¾ cup carrots sliced

¾ cup zucchini sliced

¾ cup broccoli small florets

¾ cup cauliflower small florets

¾ cup pumpkin diced

⅓ cup frozen peas

⅓ cup onion diced

1 sachet 4 cheese sauce

200ml boiling water

¼ cup 25% reduced-fat grated tasty cheese

CRUMBLE

¼ cup dried breadcrumbs

¼ cup plain flour

1 Weetbix® crushed

½ tablespoon fresh parsley chopped

1 tablespoon skim milk

1 tablespoon (15g) Flora Light® margarine melted

1 teaspoon grated parmesan cheese

DIRECTIONS

Preheat oven 180°C fan forced.

Cook all vegetables in microwave with half a cup of water on HIGH for 8 minutes. Drain and place vegetables in a medium size casserole or small lasagne dish. In a small bowl whisk cheese sauce sachet with boiling water, add grated cheese and mix until cheese has melted. Pour sauce over vegetables.

To make crumble: In a medium size mixing bowl combine all crumble ingredients, you may need to use your fingers to help create crumble texture. Sprinkle over vegetables. Bake 20 minutes or until crumble has browned on top.

Dietitian's Tip

This recipe was designed to make vegetables tasty, low in fat and kilojoules. It even will appeal to the traditional non-vegetable eater. We all need 5 serves of vegetables a day to maintain a healthy body and mind.

Nutritional Information

PER SERVE

FAT	TOTAL	4.6g
	SATURATED	1.8g
FIBRE		3.7g
PROTEIN		7.1g
CARBS		16.7g
SUGAR		3.5g
SODIUM		183mg
KILOJOULES		573 (cals 136)
GI RATING		MEDIUM

Stuffed Tomatoes

SERVES: 4

4 x 600g medium size tomatoes

cooking spray

1 teaspoon crushed garlic (in jar)

¾ cup onion small dice

¾ cup capsicum small dice

1 cup mushrooms small dice

1 tablespoon salt-reduced vegetable stock powder

½ teaspoon dried basil

2 tablespoons no-added-salt tomato paste

½ cup 25% reduced-fat grated tasty cheese

DIRECTIONS

Preheat oven 180°C fan forced.

Cut each tomato in half width ways, carefully scoop out tomato pulp, chop any firm pieces of tomato. In a medium size non-stick frypan that has been generously coated with cooking spray, sauté garlic and onion for 1 minute, toss in capsicum and mushrooms, cook 2 minutes. Add stock powder, tomato pulp, basil, tomato paste and combine well, cook 2 minutes. Spoon equal amounts into each tomato half. Place on a flat baking tray that has been coated with cooking spray then sprinkle cheese over tops. Bake 20 minutes.

VARIATION: REPLACE TOMATOES WITH 500g ZUCCHINI, CUT IN HALF LENGTH WAYS, CAREFULLY SCOOP OUT SOFT CENTRE OF ZUCCHINI AND FOLLOW RECIPE AS ABOVE.

Dietitian's Tip

Tomatoes contain lycopene a natural pigment and antioxidant that gives them their red colour. In this recipe the tomatoes have been cooked making the lycopene more efficiently absorbed into the bloodstream so it can fight free radicals and thereby slow down the effects of aging and reduced disease risk.

Nutritional Information

PER SERVE		TOMATO	ZUCCHINI
FAT	TOTAL	3.3g	3.5g
	SATURATED	1.9g	1.9g
FIBRE		3.4g	3.6g
PROTEIN		7.1g	7.1g
CARBS		6.5g	5.7g
SUGAR		5.3g	4.5g
SODIUM		115mg	107mg
KILOJOULES		353 (cals 84)	342 (cals 81)
GI RATING		TOO LOW IN CARBS TO SCORE A RATING	

Seafood

Thai Fish Curry

Thai Fish Curry

SERVES: 4

500g firm boneless
fish fillets

500g potatoes

1½ cups fresh green
beans

1 x 227g can bamboo shoots drained

cooking spray

1 teaspoon crushed ginger (in jar)

1 teaspoon crushed garlic (in jar)

1 cup carrots cut in half then sliced on angle

2 teaspoons yellow curry paste or to taste

1½ cups water

12 dried lime leaves

4 teaspoons salt-reduced vegetable
stock powder

½ cup shallots cut into 1cm slices

1 medium tomato diced

⅓ cup fresh coriander roughly chopped

1 teaspoon soy sauce 43% less salt

1 tablespoon cornflour

1 x 375ml can evaporated light milk

1 teaspoon imitation coconut essence

Dietitian's Tip
Different coloured vegetables provide different vitamins, phytochemicals and minerals including antioxidants. These fight the potentially ageing and cancer producing free radical irons produced in our body.

DIRECTIONS

Cut fish into large dice. Peel and cut potato into large dice. Cut beans in half. Cut bamboo shoots in half width ways. In a large non-stick frypan or wok (that has a lid), coat with cooking spray then sauté ginger and garlic for 30 seconds. Add fish and toss together. Cook 3 minutes. Remove fish onto a plate, leave to one side.

Recoat frypan with cooking spray toss carrots, beans and potato in pan for 3 minutes. Add yellow curry paste and stir well. Add water, lime leaves, stock powder and simmer with the lid on for 10-15 minutes or until potato is just cooked through. Add bamboo shoots, shallots, tomatoes, coriander, soy sauce and combine well. Blend cornflour with milk and essence, add to pan stirring continuously. Once boiled add fish to pan, cook 2 minutes then serve.

VARIATIONS: REPLACE FISH WITH 500g RAW SKINLESS CHICKEN BREASTS, LEAN RUMP STEAKS OR 400g TOFU DICED.

Tuna and Tomato Patties

SERVES: 6

300g potatoes

1 x 425g can tuna in spring water

1 x 180g can tuna in spring water

1 x 400g can diced tomato with capsicum
and onion

1 cup dried breadcrumbs

2 teaspoons salt-reduced
vegetable stock powder

3 tablespoons sweet
chilli sauce

cooking spray

Dietitian's Tip
Tuna in spring water provides less sodium (salt) than tuna in brine and less fat than tuna in oil. It is a healthy low kilojoule option for people with high blood pressure wanting to shed those extra kilos.

DIRECTIONS

Peel and dice potatoes, microwave on HIGH with a little water 5-6 minutes or until cooked. Drain well then mash, leave to cool. Drain tuna and break up pieces so they are not too large. Drain canned tomatoes (liquid is not required). Place all ingredients into a large mixing bowl and combine well using your hands to blend mixture together. Make 12 patties, refrigerate until required. In a large non-stick frypan generously coated with cooking spray, fry patties until browned. Before turning spray tops of patties then carefully turn and cook until browned.

Nutritional Information (F)

PER SERVE		FISH	CHICKEN	RUMP	TOFU
FAT	TOTAL	2.7g	4.7g	5.1g	7.8g
	SATURATED	1.2g	1.8g	2.4g	1.0g
FIBRE		5.3g	5.3g	5.3g	5.3g
PROTEIN		34.7g	41.1g	42.1g	22.8g
CARBS		29.1g	29.1g	29.1g	33.1g
SUGAR		14.9g	14.9g	14.9g	15.9g
SODIUM		368mg	326mg	319mg	263mg
KILOJOULES		1192(cals 284)	1374(cals 327)	1405(cals 334)	1143(272)
GI RATING		HIGH	HIGH	HIGH	HIGH

Nutritional Information (F)

PER SERVE		
FAT	TOTAL	2.5g
	SATURATED	0.6g
FIBRE		1.7g
PROTEIN		15.8g
CARBS		27.0g
SUGAR		3.4g
SODIUM		417mg
KILOJOULES		824 (Cals 196)
GI RATING		HIGH

Fish Bruschetta

SERVES: 6

6 medium size ripe tomatoes
½ salad onion finely diced
3 cloves fresh garlic finely chopped
3 tablespoons fresh basil leaves chopped
2 teaspoons virgin olive oil
2 teaspoons salt-reduced vegetable
stock powder
pepper
6 x 125g boneless fish fillets
2 tablespoons Moroccan seasoning
cooking spray
1 x 170g French bread stick

DIRECTIONS

Score or cut a small cross at the bottom of each tomato. Drop tomatoes into a large saucepan that is three quarters filled with boiling water and boil for 1 minute. Remove and cool under cold water, peel skin from tomatoes. Cut tomatoes in half then using your hands squeeze as much juice out as possible (juice is not needed). Chop tomato flesh then place into a large mixing bowl. Add onion, garlic, basil, oil, stock powder and pepper to bowl, combine well.

Coat each piece of fish with about 1 teaspoon of Moroccan seasoning, then pan fry in a non-stick frypan that has been generously coated with cooking spray for 3-4 minutes. Before turning recoat fish with cooking spray then carefully turn and cook another 3-4 minutes

or until fish is cooked through. Cut bread into 18 slices, place under griller and toast both sides. Lay 3 slices of bread on each plate then place a piece of fish on top of toast. Spread one sixth of tomato mix over fish. (If you want the topping served hot place into a small saucepan and heat before pouring over fish).

VARIATIONS: REPLACE FISH WITH 750g RAW SKINLESS CHICKEN BREASTS OR LEAN RUMP STEAKS.

Dietitian's Tip
Salt-reduced vegetable stock provides loads of taste. Too much salt in your eating plan can lead to high blood pressure, heart disease and strokes.

Nutritional Information   Ⓕ

PER SERVE		FISH	CHICKEN	RUMP
FAT	TOTAL	3.7g	5.7g	6.1g
	SATURATED	0.5g	1.1g	1.7g
FIBRE		3.2g	3.2g	3.2g
PROTEIN		26.2g	32.6g	33.6g
CARBS		19.1g	19.1g	19.1g
SUGAR		4.1g	4.1g	4.1g
SODIUM		441mg	398mg	392mg
KILOJOULES		909 (cals 216)	1092 (cals 260)	1123 (cals 267)
GI RATING		HIGH	HIGH	HIGH

Ginger Lime Fish

SERVES: 4

- 1 tablespoon (15g) Flora Light® margarine
- ½ teaspoon crushed garlic (in jar)
- ¼ cup ginger marmalade
- 2 tablespoons fresh lime juice
- 1 teaspoon salt-reduced chicken-style stock powder
- ½ teaspoon soy sauce 43% less salt
- 2 tablespoons cornflour
- 1 cup water
- cooking spray
- 4 x 150g boneless fish fillets

Dietitian's Tip
Protein is made up of small organic chemicals called amino acids. Eight of these must be obtained from the food we eat. Protein from animal sources is of greater nutritional value than plant sources because they usually contain all the essential amino acids.

DIRECTIONS

In a medium size saucepan melt margarine and sauté garlic for 15 seconds. Add marmalade, lime juice, stock powder and soy sauce, bring to boil stirring continuously. Reduce heat to slow boil for 2 minutes. Combine cornflour with water and stir into pan until boiling, using a whisk to avoid lumps. Reduce to a low heat while fish is cooking.

In a non-stick frypan that has been generously coated with cooking spray, fry fish fillets 3-4 minutes each side or until cooked (overcooking fish will make it dry). Place fish on serving plate and pour a quarter of the sauce over each piece of fish.

VARIATIONS: REPLACE FISH WITH 4 x 125g OF EITHER RAW SKINLESS CHICKEN BREASTS OR LEAN BUTTERFLY PORK STEAKS.

Nutritional Information Ⓕ

PER SERVE		FISH	CHICKEN	PORK
FAT	TOTAL	3.0g	4.8g	3.2g
	SATURATED	0.5g	1.1g	0.8g
FIBRE		0.1g	0.1g	0.1g
PROTEIN		26.5g	28.5g	30.8g
CARBS		18.6g	18.6g	18.6g
SUGAR		13.2g	13.2g	13.2g
SODIUM		356mg	291mg	287mg
KILOJOULES		885 (cals 211)	987 (cals 235)	966 (cals 230)
GI RATING		LOW	LOW	LOW

Prawn and Pineapple Yellow Curry

SERVES: 4

- 1 onion
- cooking spray
- 400g raw peeled prawns
- 1 teaspoon crushed garlic (in jar)
- 1 teaspoon crushed ginger (in jar)
- 1½ teaspoons yellow curry paste
- 1 teaspoon salt-reduced chicken-style stock powder
- 1 x 440g can pineapple pieces in natural juice
- 1 teaspoon soy sauce 43% less salt
- 2 tablespoons cornflour
- 1 x 375ml can evaporated light milk
- ¾ teaspoon imitation coconut essence

Dietitian's Tip
Annette has substituted coconut essence and evaporated light milk for coconut milk. This means a great flavour without the saturated fat and extra kilojoules.

DIRECTIONS

Peel onion, cut into quarters, then into slices. In a large non-stick frypan that has been generously coated with cooking spray, sauté prawns, onion, garlic and ginger for 2 minutes. Add curry paste and sauté 1 minute. Add stock powder, pineapple including juice and soy sauce. Blend cornflour with evaporated milk and essence, add to pan and combine well.

VARIATIONS: REPLACE PRAWNS WITH 500g SKINLESS CHICKEN BREASTS, BUTTERFLY PORK STEAKS OR 400g TOFU DICED.

Nutritional Information Ⓕ

PER SERVE		PRAWN	CHICKEN	PORK	TOFU
FAT	TOTAL	2.3g	4.6g	2.9g	7.7g
	SATURATED	1.1g	1.8g	1.4g	1.0g
FIBRE		1.7g	1.7g	1.7g	1.7g
PROTEIN		29.7g	37.4g	39.7g	19.2g
CARBS		26.8g	26.8g	26.8g	30.8g
SUGAR		23.0g	23.0g	23.0g	24.0g
SODIUM		492mg	211mg	207mg	148mg
KILOJOULES		1047 (cals 249)	1262 (cals 300)	1241 (cals 295)	1031 (cals 245)
GI RATING		MEDIUM	MEDIUM	MEDIUM	MEDIUM

Crumbed Fish with Light Cheese Sauce

Dietitian's Tip
Fish has loads of protein and is low in kilojoules and fat. The cheese sauce will help contribute to your calcium intake helping you maintain healthy bones.

SERVES: 4

1 egg white
2 tablespoons skim milk
½ cup dried breadcrumbs
4 x 150g boneless fish fillets
cooking spray

CHEESE SAUCE
1 tablespoon Flora Light® margarine
2 tablespoons plain flour
1½ cups skim milk
2 tablespoons grated parmesan cheese
1 teaspoon salt-reduced chicken-style stock powder
½ cup 25% reduced-fat grated tasty cheese
pepper to taste

DIRECTIONS

On a dinner plate beat egg white and milk together. Pour breadcrumbs onto another plate. Dip fish in egg mix then coat fish with breadcrumbs. Leave to one side.
To make sauce: In a medium size saucepan melt margarine, add flour and stir well. Slowly add milk, using a whisk to avoid lumps. Add parmesan, stock powder, grated cheese and pepper stirring continuously. Leave on a very low heat. **To cook fish:** In a large non-stick frypan that has been generously coated with cooking spray, cook fish fillets for 3 minutes. Coat top of fish generously with cooking spray, then turn and cook a further 3 minutes or until fish is cooked through. Place on serving plates and pour cheese sauce over top.

Nutritional Information ⓕ

PER SERVE		
FAT	TOTAL	4.8g
	SATURATED	2.4g
FIBRE		0.5g
PROTEIN		35.2g
CARBS		11.9g
SUGAR		4.4g
SODIUM		405mg
KILOJOULES		975 (cals 232)
GI RATING		LOW

Curried Tuna Potato Salad

Dietitian's Tip
Tuna and eggs provide lots of protein required for your body to grow and repair damage that occurs in the tissues.

SERVES: 6

1 kilo new potatoes cut into quarters
1 x 425g can tuna in spring water
3 hard-boiled eggs sliced
½ cup shallots sliced
½ cup celery sliced
1 tablespoon curry powder
1 cup 97% fat-free mayonnaise
pepper

DIRECTIONS

Boil potatoes in a microwave or saucepan until just cooked. Rinse and leave potatoes to cool. Drain tuna and break up pieces so that they are not too large. In a large mixing bowl place potatoes, tuna, sliced egg, shallots and celery. Combine curry powder with mayonnaise and add to bowl. Gently fold all ingredients until well combined. Pepper to taste. Refrigerate until required.

VARIATIONS: REPLACE POTATO WITH 4 CUPS COOKED PASTA (PENNE, SPIRAL, MACARONI ETC) OR REPLACE TUNA WITH PINK SALMON OR OMIT CURRY POWDER FOR PLAIN TUNA POTATO SALAD.

Nutritional Information ⓕ

PER SERVE		TUNA POTATO	TUNA PASTA	SALMON POTATO
FAT	TOTAL	4.6g	4.8g	6.5g
	SATURATED	1.3g	1.3g	1.7g
FIBRE		3.8g	2.3g	3.8g
PROTEIN		19.9g	19.9g	18.5g
CARBS		36.4g	38.7g	36.4g
SUGAR		12.6g	11.8g	12.6g
SODIUM		423mg	474mg	666mg
KILOJOULES		1155 (cals 275)	1190 (cals 283)	1202 (cals 286)
GI RATING		HIGH	LOW	HIGH

Tuna Tomato Casserole

SERVES: 4

cooking spray

1 teaspoon crushed garlic (in jar)

1 medium onion diced

¾ cup green capsicum diced

1 cup carrots cut in half then thinly sliced

1 cup celery sliced

1 x 425g can tuna in spring water (drained)

1 x 180g can tuna in spring water (drained)

2 teaspoons salt-reduced vegetable stock powder

1 teaspoon dried dill

2 tablespoons no-added-salt tomato paste

1 x 420g can salt-reduced tomato soup

BREAD TOP

2 x 40g long bread rolls

1 teaspoon crushed garlic (in jar)

1 tablespoon (15g) Flora Light® margarine

1 tablespoon grated parmesan cheese

paprika

DIRECTIONS

In a large non-stick saucepan that has been coated with cooking spray, sauté garlic, onion, capsicum, carrot and celery for 5 minutes. Drain tuna and break up so that pieces are not too large, add to pan. Mix in stock powder, dill, tomato paste and soup, stirring well. Bring to boil then reduce to a slow boil for 3 minutes or until vegetables are cooked to your liking.

To make bread top: Cut each bread roll into six slices. In a small bowl combine garlic and margarine. Spread evenly over the bread slices. Sprinkle parmesan cheese over top. Sprinkle a light coating of paprika over each slice. Place under griller until top is toasted. Place three slices on top of each serve.

Dietitian's Tip
Tuna is naturally low in fat and saturated fat when compared to other protein foods and provides omega-3 fatty acids. It is an excellent food for people with diabetes and heart disease.

Nutritional Information   Ⓕ

PER SERVE		WITH BREAD	W/OUT BREAD
FAT	TOTAL	6.2g	3.0g
	SATURATED	1.9g	1.1g
FIBRE		2.9g	2.0g
PROTEIN		32.1g	29.5g
CARBS		25.8g	15.1g
SUGAR		12.9g	12.1g
SODIUM		455mg	300mg
KILOJOULES		1214 (cals 289)	871 (cals 207)
GI RATING		MEDIUM	MEDIUM

Chicken Enchiladas

Chicken Enchiladas

SERVES: 6

500g raw skinless chicken breast
cooking spray
1 teaspoon crushed garlic (in jar)
1 cup green capsicum diced
1 onion finely diced
1 cup fresh tomatoes diced
⅛ teaspoon chilli powder or to taste
1 teaspoon cumin
1 teaspoon dried coriander
2 teaspoons salt-reduced chicken-style
stock powder
1 x 300g jar spicy bean salsa
¼ cup water
12 white corn tortilla wraps (Diego's®)
¾ cup 25% reduced-fat grated tasty cheese

DIRECTIONS

Preheat oven 180°C fan forced. Cut chicken into small dice. In a large non-stick frypan that has been generously coated with cooking spray, sauté chicken and garlic for 5 minutes. Toss in capsicum and onion and cook a further 3 minutes. Add all remaining ingredients except tortilla wraps and cheese and combine well. When boiled reduce to a slow boil for 3 minutes.

To prepare and soften wraps follow instructions on back of tortilla packet. Place one twelfth of the filling at one end of the wrap and roll up. Repeat for eleven remaining wraps. Place on a large flat baking tray that has been coated with cooking spray, placing folded side down. Sprinkle an even amount of grated cheese on top of each wrap. Bake 20-25 minutes.

VARIATIONS: REPLACE CHICKEN WITH 500g RAW LEAN RUMP STEAKS OR 400g TOFU SMALL DICE. FOOTNOTE: THIS IS A GLUTEN FREE RECIPE.

> *Dietitian's Tip*
> People with coeliac disease or those requiring gluten free diets can use tortillas as they are made from cornflour. However it is always advisable to ensure that "gluten free" is written on the label of the product.

Curry in a Hurry

SERVES: 6

1 whole BBQ chicken
1 onion diced
1 x 500g packet frozen Winter Vegetables (McCain®)
1 cup water
2 cups skim milk
½ sachet (¼ cup) Dutch Curry & Rice soup mix
1 tablespoon curry powder
2 teaspoons salt-reduced chicken-style stock powder

DIRECTIONS

Remove all skin and bone from chicken. Dice or shred flesh. Microwave onion and frozen vegetables with 1 cup of water on HIGH for 5 minutes. In a large saucepan combine milk, soup mix, curry powder and stock powder stirring continuously until boiling. Add vegetables and water to mix, combine well. Fold in chicken, bring back to boil, reduce to slow boil and cook a further 2-3 minutes.

VARIATION: REPLACE WINTER FROZEN VEGETABLES WITH ANY FROZEN MIXED VEGETABLES OF YOUR CHOICE.

> *Dietitian's Tip*
> Quick, nutritious meal that is high in protein and contains added calcium from the milk with vitamins, minerals and fibre from the vegetables. This is a great choice for people with diabetes and heart disease.

Nutritional Information ⒡

PER SERVE		CHICKEN	RUMP	TOFU
FAT	TOTAL	6.8g	7.1g	8.9g
	SATURATED	2.8g	3.3g	2.3g
FIBRE		6.8g	6.8g	6.8g
PROTEIN		30.3g	31.0g	18.2g
CARBS		39.8g	39.8g	42.5g
SUGAR		8.0g	8.0g	8.6g
SODIUM		419mg	415mg	377mg
KILOJOULES		1491 (cals 355)	1512 (360)	1337 (cals 318)
GI RATING		LOW	LOW	LOW

Nutritional Information ⒡

PER SERVE		
FAT	TOTAL	14.1g
	SATURATED	4.1g
FIBRE		5.4g
PROTEIN		26.0g
CARBS		14.8g
SUGAR		8.0g
SODIUM		399mg
KILOJOULES		1210 (cals 288)
GI RATING		MEDIUM

Honey Mustard Chicken

SERVES: 4

- 1 cup carrots sliced
- 1 cup broccoli florets
- 1 cup celery sliced
- cooking spray
- 500g raw skinless chicken breast diced
- 1 teaspoon crushed garlic (in jar)
- 1 small onion diced
- 2 teaspoons salt-reduced chicken-style stock powder
- 4 tablespoons Dijon mustard (in jar)
- 2 tablespoons honey
- 1 tablespoon cornflour
- 1 x 375ml can evaporated light milk
- pepper

Dietitian's Tip
Honey adds a unique sweet flavour to foods. People with diabetes are free to add small amounts of honey to healthy recipes. This recipe contains loads of vegetables and lean meat - it is a healthy choice.

DIRECTIONS

Microwave carrots, broccoli and celery with a little water on HIGH for 5 minutes. In a large non-stick frypan that has been generously coated with cooking spray, sauté chicken and garlic for 3 minutes. Add onion and cook 2 minutes. Drain vegetables and add to pan, stir into pan, cook 2 minutes. Add stock powder, mustard and honey, mix well. Blend cornflour with evaporated milk, pour into pan stirring continuously until boiled. Add pepper to taste.

VARIATIONS: REPLACE CHICKEN WITH 500g RAW LEAN RUMP STEAK OR PORK BUTTERFLY STEAK OR 400g TOFU DICED.

Nutritional Information Ⓕ

PER SERVE		CHICKEN	RUMP	PORK	TOFU
FAT	TOTAL	4.8g	5.2g	3.2g	8.0g
	SATURATED	1.8g	2.4g	1.4g	1.0g
FIBRE		3.1g	3.1g	3.1g	3.1g
PROTEIN		38.5g	39.5g	40.7g	20.2g
CARBS		25.0g	25.0g	25.0g	29.0g
SUGAR		22.7g	22.7g	22.7g	23.7g
SODIUM		331mg	325mg	327mg	268mg
KILOJOULES		1248(cals297)	1279(cals305)	1227(cals292)	1017(cals242)
GI RATING		LOW	LOW	LOW	LOW

Chicken Cordon Bleu

SERVES: 4

- 4 x 125g raw skinless chicken breasts
- ¼ cup shallots cut into 1cm slices
- 60g 97% fat-free ham (approx 4 slices) cut in strips
- 4 x 20g slices Bega Super Slim® cheese
- toothpicks
- 1 egg white
- 2 tablespoons skim milk
- ½ cup dried breadcrumbs
- cooking spray

Dietitian's Tip
Annette's use of low fat ham, cheese and milk reduces the total fat and saturated fat content of Chicken Cordon Bleu. This recipe is ideal for those at risk of heart disease as well as people with diabetes.

DIRECTIONS

Preheat oven 180°C fan forced. Using a sharp knife, make a pocket lengthways inside each chicken breast (don't cut all the way through). Use your finger to widen and open the hole to allow for filling. Place a quarter of shallots and ham in centre of one cheese slice, roll up cheese and place into a breast, pushing deep into pocket. Seal opening with toothpicks. Repeat this process for remaining chicken breasts. In a medium size mixing bowl beat egg white with milk. Place breadcrumbs on a large dinner plate, dip each breast into egg mix, and coat with breadcrumbs. Place on a baking tray that has been generously coated with cooking spray, spray tops of chicken. Bake 20-25 minutes or until chicken is cooked through.

VARIATION: REPLACE CHICKEN WITH LEAN VEAL LEG STEAKS.

Nutritional Information Ⓕ

PER SERVE		CHICKEN	VEAL
FAT	TOTAL	5.8g	3.3g
	SATURATED	2.3g	1.7g
FIBRE		0.5g	0.5g
PROTEIN		38.5g	36.6g
CARBS		9.0g	8.9g
SUGAR		2.0g	2.0g
SODIUM		504mg	545mg
KILOJOULES		1018 (cals 242)	1008 (cals 240)
GI RATING		TOO LOW IN CARBS TO SCORE A RATING	

Creamy Chicken Crumble

SERVES: 6

FILLING: 1 cup carrots diced
1 cup green beans sliced
cooking spray
500g raw skinless chicken
breast diced
1 teaspoon crushed garlic (in jar)
1 onion diced
1 x 310g can creamed corn
1 sachet 98% fat-free chicken & vegetable Cup-a-Soup
1 teaspoon salt-reduced chicken-style stock powder
1 tablespoon fresh parsley chopped
1 x 30g sachet 4 cheese sauce (Continental®)
1 cup boiling water
CRUMBLE: ½ cup dried breadcrumbs
½ cup plain flour
2 tablespoons grated parmesan cheese
1 tablespoon fresh parsley chopped
2 Weet-bix® crushed
2 tablespoons skim milk
4 tablespoons (60g) Flora Light® margarine melted

Dietitian's Tip
A high fibre, tasty chicken dish. It is recommended we have 30g of fibre a day to provide us with a healthy gastrointestinal system and reduce the risk of bowel cancer.

DIRECTIONS

Preheat oven 180°C fan forced. **To make filling:** Microwave carrots and beans in a little water on HIGH for 5 minutes. Generously coat a large saucepan with cooking spray and sauté chicken with garlic for 3 minutes. Add onion and cook 2 minutes. Add corn, cooked vegetables, soup mix, stock powder and parsley. Blend cheese sauce sachet with 1 cup boiling water. Add to pot, combine well. Pour filling into large casserole or lasagne dish. **To make crumble:** Combine all ingredients. You may need to use your hands to get a crumbled texture. Sprinkle evenly over top of filling. Bake 40-45 minutes.

VARIATION: REPLACE CHICKEN WITH 2 x 425g CANS TUNA IN SPRING WATER DRAINED.

Nutritional Information Ⓕ

PER SERVE		CHICKEN	TUNA
FAT	TOTAL	8.7g	9.2g
	SATURATED	2.1g	2.5g
FIBRE		5.2g	5.2g
PROTEIN		25.1g	29.4g
CARBS		28.1g	28.1g
SUGAR		5.4g	5.4g
SODIUM		458mg	488mg
KILOJOULES		1223 (cals 291)	1316 (cals 313)
GI RATING		MEDIUM	MEDIUM

Mango Lime Chicken

SERVES: 4

1 x 420g can mango slices in natural juice
cooking spray
1 teaspoon crushed garlic (in jar)
500g raw skinless chicken breast diced
¼ cup shallots sliced
2 tablespoons fresh lime juice
1 teaspoon lime rind grated
2 teaspoons salt-reduced chicken-style stock powder
2 teaspoons sugar
1 tablespoon cornflour
1 cup evaporated light milk

Dietitian's Tip
The recommended daily intake of vitamin C for adult Australians is 30mg per day. Mango is a rich source of vitamin C providing 30mg per 100g making it ideal for people who enjoy healthy refreshing fruit.

DIRECTIONS

Drain mangoes keeping juice to add later. Cut mangoes into large dice. In a large non-stick frypan that has been generously coated with cooking spray, sauté garlic and chicken until almost cooked. Add shallots, lime juice, rind, stock powder, sugar, cook 1 minute. Add mango and mango juice. Combine cornflour with evaporated milk, add to pan stirring continuously until boiling and sauce thickens.

VARIATION: REPLACE CHICKEN WITH 500g RAW BONELESS FISH FILLETS DICED.

Nutritional Information Ⓕ

PER SERVE		CHICKEN	FISH
FAT	TOTAL	4.5g	2.5g
	SATURATED	1.8g	1.2g
FIBRE		1.1g	1.1g
PROTEIN		37.1g	30.7g
CARBS		25.3g	25.3g
SUGAR		23.3g	23.3g
SODIUM		164mg	204mg
KILOJOULES		1230 (cals 293)	1048 (cals 250)
GI RATING		LOW	LOW

Stuffed Apricot Chicken

SERVES: 4

1 cup cooked Basmati rice
½ cup dried apricots small dice
1 teaspoon salt-reduced chicken-style stock powder
¼ cup shallots sliced
1½ tablespoons Thai chilli stir fry paste
4 x 125g raw skinless chicken breasts
toothpicks
cooking spray
SAUCE: ½ teaspoon crushed ginger (in jar)
¼ cup brandy
1 cup apricot nectar
1 teaspoon salt-reduced chicken-style stock powder
2 teaspoons cornflour
¼ cup water

> **Dietitian's Tip**
> Basmati rice has a lower GI than other varieties, making it a suitable choice for people with diabetes or interested in good health.

DIRECTIONS

Preheat oven 180°C fan forced. Combine rice, apricots, stock powder, shallots and chilli paste together. Using a sharp knife, make a pocket lengthways inside each chicken breast (don't cut all the way through). Use your finger to widen and open the hole to allow for filling. Spoon a quarter of the mixture into each breast pocket. Push filling deep into breast, then seal opening with toothpicks. Place chicken onto a baking tray that has been generously coated with cooking spray. Spray over top of chicken. Bake 25-30 minutes or until chicken is cooked through.

To make sauce: In a small saucepan that has been coated with cooking spray, sauté ginger for 15 seconds, add brandy. Using a whisk stir in apricot nectar and stock powder. Blend cornflour with water and whisk into pot, bring to boil. Pour a quarter of sauce over top of each chicken breast.

VARIATION: FOR MANGO CHICKEN REPLACE DRIED APRICOTS WITH DRIED MANGO AND APRICOT NECTAR WITH MANGO NECTAR.

Nutritional Information ⓕ

PER SERVE		
FAT	TOTAL	3.5g
	SATURATED	0.9g
FIBRE		1.7g
PROTEIN		29.9g
CARBS		25.8g
SUGAR		17.3g
SODIUM		202mg
KILOJOULES		1202 (cals 286)
GI RATING		LOW

Mexican Chicken Stack

SERVES: 6

cooking spray
1 cup raw Basmati rice
1 tablespoon salt-reduced chicken-style stock powder
2½ cups boiling water
1½ teaspoons Cajun seasoning
1½ teaspoons cumin
500g raw skinless chicken breast
1 x 420g can Mexi beans
1 teaspoon crushed garlic (in jar)
1 x 425g can no-added-salt tomato puree
1 cup each of capsicum, celery & onion finely diced
1 cup each of very small florets of broccoli & cauliflower
½ cup 25% reduced-fat grated tasty cheese

> **Dietitian's Tip**
> Beans are packed with soluble fibre, which slows down stomach emptying, therefore helping people to feel full for longer after eating. An excellent choice of food for people with diabetes.

DIRECTIONS

In a large saucepan (that has a lid), generously coat base with cooking spray, sauté rice and stock powder for 1 minute. Add boiling water, once boiling put lid on and reduce to a slow boil for 15 minutes. Do not remove lid whilst cooking. Remove from heat and give it a good stir, leave to one side. Mix Cajun seasoning and cumin together and coat over chicken. In a non-stick frypan that has been generously coated with cooking spray, cook chicken breasts. Cut into small dice, leave to one side. Using a food processor or Bamix® puree Mexi beans until smooth paste. Combine garlic with tomato puree, leave to one side. Cook vegetables in a microwave dish with a little water on HIGH for 4 minutes, drain.

To assemble stack: Place cooked rice in the centre of 6 dinner plates making a round shape the size of a side plate. Spread an equal amount of bean mix over top of rice then top with chopped chicken. Place vegetables over chicken then pour tomato puree over top. Sprinkle cheese evenly over puree. Microwave each plate 3-4 minutes on HIGH.

VARIATIONS: REPLACE CHICKEN WITH RAW LEAN RUMP STEAK OR FOR A VEGETARIAN VERSION REPLACE CHICKEN WITH 1 x 420g CAN 4 BEAN MIX DRAINED AND WASHED.

Nutritional Information ⓕ

PER SERVE		CHICKEN	RUMP	VEGETARIAN
FAT	TOTAL	5.1g	5.4g	3.5g
	SATURATED	2.1g	2.5g	1.7g
FIBRE		6.3g	6.3g	9.8g
PROTEIN		28.7g	29.3g	13.2g
CARBS		25.4g	25.4g	32.4g
SUGAR		6.6g	6.6g	7.5g
SODIUM		486mg	482mg	549mg
KILOJOULES		1103 (cals 263)	1124 (cals 268)	928 (cals221)
GI RATING		LOW	LOW	LOW

Chicken Pesto Pasta

SERVES: 6

3⅓ cups (300g) raw penne pasta

PESTO

2 teaspoons pine nuts
½ teaspoon crushed garlic (in jar)
2 teaspoons grated parmesan cheese
2 tablespoons water
½ teaspoon salt-reduced vegetable stock powder
½ bunch (45g) fresh basil leaves
1 teaspoon virgin olive oil

SAUCE

500g raw skinless chicken breast
cooking spray
2 teaspoons crushed garlic (in jar)
1 onion diced
2 cups mushrooms sliced
4 tablespoons no-added-salt tomato paste
2 teaspoons salt-reduced chicken-style stock powder
2 tablespoons cornflour
½ cup skim milk
1 x 375ml can evaporated light milk
pepper

DIRECTIONS

Cook pasta following instructions on pasta packet, leave to one side.

To make pesto: Place pine nuts on a sheet of aluminium foil and brown under griller (be careful as they burn easily). Place all pesto ingredients into either a small blender or use a Bamix® and blend until a paste is made. Leave to one side.

To make sauce: Cut chicken breasts into strips. In a large non-stick frypan that has been coated generously with

cooking spray, sauté garlic and chicken until browned. Add onion and cook 2 minutes. Toss in mushrooms and cook a further 2 minutes. Add tomato paste, stock powder and pesto, mix well. Combine cornflour with skim milk, pour into pan with evaporated milk, bring to boil, pepper to taste. Add cooked pasta to pan, combine well.

VARIATIONS: REPLACE CHICKEN WITH 500g RAW LEAN RUMP STEAKS, LEAN LAMB LEG STEAKS OR 500g RAW PEELED PRAWNS.

Dietitian's Tip
Pasta is a low GI carbohydrate food. However it is still important that people with diabetes moderate their serving sizes to minimise the possibility of blood sugars going up and down. This serving size, would be ideal for most people with diabetes.

Nutritional Information (F)

PER SERVE		CHICKEN	RUMP	LAMB	PRAWN
FAT	TOTAL	5.6g	5.8g	5.5g	4.1g
	SATURATED	1.7g	2.1g	2.0g	1.2g
FIBRE		3.1g	3.1g	3.1g	3.1g
PROTEIN		32.7g	33.4g	32.9g	31.0g
CARBS		46.4g	46.4g	46.4g	46.4g
SUGAR		10.4g	10.4g	10.4g	10.4g
SODIUM		145mg	141mg	153mg	391mg
KILOJOULES		1554(cals 370)	1574(cals 375)	1554(cals 370)	1472(cals 350)
GI RATING		LOW	LOW	LOW	LOW

Nutritional Information (F)

PER SERVE		CHICKEN	PORK
FAT	TOTAL	3.0g	1.3g
	SATURATED	0.8g	0.4g
FIBRE		1.2g	1.2g
PROTEIN		28.9g	31.2g
CARBS		22.3g	22.3g
SUGAR		19.6g	19.6g
SODIUM		77mg	72mg
KILOJOULES		1104 (cals 263)	1083 (cals 258)
GI RATING		MEDIUM	MEDIUM

Chicken with Black Cherry Sauce

Dietitian's Tip
Brandy and other alcoholic drinks are used in cooking to provide added flavour. Cooking evaporates off the alcohol making it no longer "alcoholic".

SERVES: 6

1 x 425g can black cherries drained
cooking spray
4 x 125g raw skinless chicken breasts
¼ cup brandy
1 teaspoon salt-reduced chicken-style stock powder
1 tablespoon cornflour
1 cup unsweetened grape juice

DIRECTIONS

Cut cherries in half. In a large non-stick frypan that has been generously coated with cooking spray, fry chicken until cooked. Remove from pan, leave to one side. Pour brandy into frypan, add cherries and stock powder stirring well. Blend cornflour with grape juice, add to pan stirring until sauce boils. Place chicken back into pan and reheat covering with sauce.

VARIATION: REPLACE CHICKEN WITH 500g RAW LEAN BUTTERFLY PORK STEAKS.

Satay Pork Burger

Satay Pork Burger

SERVES: 6

SATAY SAUCE

2½ tablespoons peanut butter

½ cup 97% fat-free mayonnaise

1 teaspoon red curry paste

1½ teaspoons soy sauce 43% less salt

BURGER

500g lean pork mince

1 egg white

2 teaspoons salt-reduced chicken-style stock powder

1 teaspoon crushed garlic (in jar)

1 teaspoon crushed ginger (in jar)

1 tablespoon Thai seasoning

2 teaspoons lemongrass (in jar)

cooking spray

6 x 50g multi-grain bread rolls

3 small tomatoes sliced

24 slices cucumber

3 cups lettuce shredded

> **Dietitian's Tip**
> Peanuts are high in protein and mono and polyunsaturated fats and low in saturated fat (18%). These qualities make it a great food for people with diabetes and heart disease.

DIRECTIONS

To make satay sauce: In a small mixing bowl combine satay sauce ingredients mixing well.

To make burger: In a large mixing bowl combine mince, egg white, stock powder, garlic, ginger, Thai seasoning and lemongrass. Use your hands to combine mixture well. Divide into 6 round shaped burger patties. In a large non-stick frypan that has been generously coated with cooking spray, fry burgers until cooked on both sides.

To assemble burger: Cut rolls in half, grill until toasted brown. Place salad on base of bun then top with burger and a sixth of satay sauce, place lid on top.

VARIATIONS: OMIT BREAD ROLL AND HAVE BURGER AND SALAD ON THEIR OWN WITH SAUCE OR REPLACE PORK MINCE WITH RAW LEAN CHICKEN MINCE OR VERY LEAN BEEF MINCE.

BURGER PATTY SUITABLE TO BE FROZEN

Symple Beef Casserole

SERVES: 6

750g lean stewing steak diced

¼ cup plain flour

cooking spray

1 teaspoon crushed garlic (in jar)

1 large onion sliced

1½ cups carrot thickly sliced

¾ cup each of parsnip and swede diced

1 cup celery sliced

2 cups water

2 tablespoons Worcestershire sauce

4 teaspoons salt-reduced chicken-style stock powder

4 dried bay leaves

¾ teaspoon each of dried rosemary and thyme

1 x 400g can no-added-salt chopped tomatoes

⅓ cup fruit chutney (in jar)

pepper to taste

3 tablespoons Gravox® Lite Supreme

¼ cup water

> **Dietitian's Tip**
> Tofu contains active phytochemicals called isoflavones geniste. Research suggests that isoflavones decrease LDL cholesterol (the bad) and increase HDL cholesterol (the good) - especially in women. This helps to prevent heart disease.

DIRECTIONS

Preheat oven 180°C fan forced. In a large bowl coat steak with flour. Place pieces of steak into a large non-stick frypan that has been generously coated with cooking spray and brown. Place meat and all other ingredients into a large casserole dish (10 cup), except Gravox and ¼ cup water, combine well, place lid on top, cook 1 hour 15 minutes, then combine Gravox powder with a ¼ cup of water and mix into casserole. Place back into oven for a further 15 minutes or until vegetables are cooked to your liking.

VARIATIONS: REPLACE STEAK WITH 750g RAW LEAN LAMB LEG STEAKS, SKINLESS CHICKEN BREAST OR 400g TOFU DICED.

Nutritional Information   Ⓕ

PER SERVE		PORK	CHICKEN	BEEF	PORK PATTY ONLY
FAT	TOTAL	12.7g	13.6g	12.6g	10.6g
	SATURATED	3.1g	3.0g	3.4g	2.9g
FIBRE		5.4g	5.4g	5.4g	2.3g
PROTEIN		25.5g	24.8g	25.7g	20.6g
CARBS		33.8g	33.8g	33.8g	8.6g
SUGAR		9.2g	9.2g	9.2g	7.2g
SODIUM		660mg	671mg	659mg	375mg
KILOJOULES		1477(cals 352)	1499(cals 357)	1478(cals 352)	889(cals 212)
GI RATING		MEDIUM	MEDIUM	MEDIUM	MEDIUM

Nutritional Information   Ⓕ

PER SERVE		STEAK	LAMB	CHICKEN	TOFU
FAT	TOTAL	4.0g	3.1g	3.2g	4.3g
	SATURATED	1.5g	1.3g	0.8g	0g
FIBRE		3.7g	3.7g	3.7g	3.7g
PROTEIN		28.5g	31.4g	31.1g	9.5g
CARBS		20.5g	20.5g	20.5g	23.2g
SUGAR		13.1g	13.1g	13.1g	13.7g
SODIUM		229mg	228mg	217mg	152mg
KILOJOULES		977(cals 233)	993(cals 236)	993(cals 236)	644(cals 153)
GI RATING		MEDIUM	MEDIUM	MEDIUM	MEDIUM

Chinese Beef

SERVES: 4

cooking spray

500g raw lean rump steak cut into strips

1 teaspoon each of crushed garlic & ginger (in jar)

1 onion sliced

1½ cups small cauliflower florets

1 cup red capsicum sliced

1 cup (95g) snow peas

1 x 227g can water chestnuts drained

5 tablespoons teriyaki marinade sauce

2 teaspoons soy sauce 43% less salt

2 teaspoons salt-reduced chicken-style stock powder

1 tablespoon cornflour

1 cup water

DIRECTIONS

In a large non-stick frypan or wok that has been generously coated with cooking spray, sauté steak with garlic and ginger until browned. Add onion and cauliflower and cook 3 minutes stirring frequently. Place capsicum, snow peas and water chestnuts into pan and sauté until cooked to your liking. Add marinade, soy sauce and stock powder to pan and stir well with meat. Blend cornflour with water, pour into pan and stir well until boiled.

VARIATIONS: REPLACE RUMP WITH EITHER 500g LAMB LEG STEAKS, SKINLESS CHICKEN BREASTS OR 400g TOFU DICED.

Dietitian's Tip
Even though reduced salt products are used in this recipe it is higher in sodium (salt) than generally recommended for people with diabetes. However traditional recipes for stir fry are much higher in sodium thus making this a better option.

Nutritional Information ⒡

PER SERVE		RUMP	LAMB	CHICKEN	TOFU
FAT	TOTAL	3.8g	3.3g	3.4g	6.6g
	SATURATED	1.4g	1.3g	0.8g	0g
FIBRE		3.0g	3.0g	3.0g	3.0g
PROTEIN		33.0g	32.3g	32.0g	13.7g
CARBS		17.2g	17.2g	17.2g	21.2g
SUGAR		5.2g	5.2g	5.2g	6.3g
SODIUM		552mg	570mg	558mg	496mg
KILOJOULES		986(cals 235)	959(cals 228)	955(cals 227)	724(cals 172)
GI RATING		MEDIUM	MEDIUM	MEDIUM	MEDIUM

Steak with Blue Cheese Sauce

SERVES: 4

4 x 125g raw lean rump steaks

cooking spray

1 teaspoon crushed garlic (in jar)

¼ cup shallots sliced

2 tablespoons brandy

75g blue vein cheese

2 teaspoons salt-reduced chicken-style stock powder

2 tablespoons cornflour

1 x 375ml can evaporated light milk

pepper

DIRECTIONS

Cut as much fat from steak as possible. In a small non-stick saucepan that has been coated with cooking spray, sauté garlic and shallots for 1 minute, pour in brandy and cook 30 seconds. Add cheese and stock powder, stir until cheese has melted. Combine cornflour with evaporated milk and pour into pot. Stir continuously until boiled and thickened, pepper to taste. Leave to one side. Coat a large non-stick frypan generously with cooking spray and fry steaks to your liking. Place steaks onto dinner plates and pour reheated cheese sauce over top.

Dietitian's Tip
Coating the saucepan with cooking spray minimises the amount of fat required to saute vegetables. This lowers the total fat and kilojoule content of the meal making it a suitable cooking style for weight loss.

Nutritional Information ⒡

PER SERVE		
FAT	TOTAL	11.5g
	SATURATED	6.6g
FIBRE		0.2g
PROTEIN		47.0g
CARBS		14.6g
SUGAR		11.2g
SODIUM		380mg
KILOJOULES		1538 (cals 366)
GI RATING		LOW

Spaghetti Bake

SERVES: 6

4½ cups cooked spaghetti strands (300g raw weight)

cooking spray

2 teaspoons crushed garlic (in jar)

1 onion diced

500g very lean beef mince

¾ cup carrot grated

¾ cup celery thinly sliced

¾ cup capsicum diced

2 x 400g cans no-added-salt chopped tomatoes

¾ cup no-added-salt tomato paste

1 tablespoon salt-reduced chicken-style stock powder

1 teaspoon dried basil

2 tablespoons grated parmesan cheese

pepper to taste

¾ cup 25% reduced-fat grated tasty cheese

DIRECTIONS

Preheat oven 180°C fan forced.

To cook pasta follow instructions on pasta packet, leave to one side. In a large non-stick frypan that has been generously coated with cooking spray, sauté garlic and onion for 1 minute. Add mince and combine. Once mince is cooked add carrot, celery and capsicum, cook 3 minutes. Stir all remaining ingredients except pasta and grated cheese into mince. Bring to boil then reduce to a slow boil and cook 5 minutes. Fold cooked spaghetti into mixture combining well with mince sauce, pour into a large lasagne dish that has been coated with cooking spray. Sprinkle grated cheese over top. Bake 35 minutes.

VARIATION: FOR A VEGETARIAN VERSION REPLACE CHICKEN STOCK WITH VEGETABLE STOCK POWDER AND REPLACE BEEF MINCE WITH 150g (1 BOX) TVP VEGE-MINCE. TO PREPARE TVP VEGE-MINCE FOLLOW INSTRUCTIONS ON BOX AND ADD WHEN ADDING CHOPPED TOMATOES.

Dietitian's Tip
Spaghetti is pasta and as such has a low GI. The carbohydrate content is high so the serving size that is recommended in this recipe is ideal for most people with diabetes and those aiming to maintain a healthy weight or lose weight.

Nutritional Information   Ⓕ

PER SERVE		BEEF	VEGETARIAN
FAT	TOTAL	11.2g	5.5g
	SATURATED	5.3g	2.9g
FIBRE		7.0g	7.9g
PROTEIN		30.9g	17.8g
CARBS		46.5g	48.5g
SUGAR		10.0g	10.7g
SODIUM		263mg	366mg
KILOJOULES		1732 (cals 412)	1340 (cals 319)
GI RATING		LOW	LOW

Beef Goulash

SERVES: 4

cooking spray
500g raw lean rump steak large dice
1 teaspoon crushed garlic (in jar)
1½ cups carrots thickly sliced
1½ cups capsicum large dice
1½ cups cauliflower small florets
1 onion diced
1½ cups water
1 x 420g can salt-reduced tomato soup
2 tablespoons no-added-salt tomato paste
2 tablespoons sweet paprika
1 teaspoon cumin
1 tablespoon salt-reduced chicken-style stock powder
pepper to taste
2 teaspoons cornflour

Dietitian's Tip
Red meat is the best source of iron. Iron forms part of the haemoglobin molecule (red blood cell) that carries oxygen from our lungs to all areas of our body.

DIRECTIONS

In a large non-stick frypan (with a lid) that has been generously coated with cooking spray, sauté steak and garlic until browned. Add carrots, capsicum, cauliflower, onion and 1 cup of the water and mix together. Place lid on and bring to boil, reduce to a moderate boil for 5 minutes. Add soup, tomato paste, paprika, cumin, stock powder, pepper and stir well. Place lid back on, slow boil for 10 minutes or until vegetables are cooked to your liking. Blend cornflour with remaining half cup of water, add to pan stirring continuously until boiling and sauce has thickened.

VARIATIONS: REPLACE RUMP WITH EITHER 500g RAW SKINLESS CHICKEN BREAST, LEAN LEG LAMB STEAK OR 400g TOFU DICED.

Nutritional Information ⓕ

PER SERVE		RUMP	CHICKEN	LAMB	TOFU
FAT	TOTAL	4.2g	3.8g	3.7g	7.0g
	SATURATED	1.4g	0.8g	1.3g	0g
FIBRE		2.7g	2.7g	2.7g	2.7g
PROTEIN		32.5g	31.5g	31.7g	13.2g
CARBS		15.4g	15.4g	15.4g	19.4g
SUGAR		10.6g	10.6g	10.6g	11.6g
SODIUM		242mg	248mg	259mg	185mg
KILOJOULES		943(cals 225)	912(cals 217)	912(cals 217)	681(cals 162)
GI RATING		LOW	LOW	LOW	LOW

Asian Lamb Potato Curry

SERVES: 4

500g potatoes
600g raw lean lamb leg steaks
cooking spray
1 teaspoon crushed garlic (in jar)
1 onion diced
1 tablespoon massaman curry paste
1 teaspoon turmeric
½ teaspoon each of cumin and cinnamon
1 tablespoon salt-reduced chicken-style stock powder
1¾ cups water
1 teaspoon fish sauce
2 teaspoons soy sauce 43% less salt
2 tablespoons cornflour
¼ cup water

Dietitian's Tip
Research into the health benefits of garlic suggests it is beneficial in many medical conditions including high blood pressure, the common cold, cancer, and bacterial and fungal infections.

DIRECTIONS

Peel and cut potato and lamb into large dice. Generously coat a large saucepan (with a lid) with cooking spray and sauté lamb and garlic until meat has browned. Add onion, curry paste, turmeric, cumin, cinnamon and stock powder, combine well. Cook 1 minute. Add potatoes, stir well. Add water, fish and soy sauce to pot. Once boiled put lid on, reduce to a medium boil for 15 minutes. Remove lid and cook 5 minutes or until potato is cooked. Combine cornflour with a quarter cup of water, add to pot stirring well until sauce has boiled and thickened.

VARIATIONS: REPLACE LAMB WITH LEAN RUMP STEAK, SKINLESS CHICKEN BREAST OR 400g TOFU DICED.

Nutritional Information ⓕ

PER SERVE		LAMB	CHICKEN	RUMP	TOFU
FAT	TOTAL	3.7g	4.3g	3.9g	6.4g
	SATURATED	1.5g	1.7g	0.9g	0g
FIBRE		3.2g	3.2g	3.2g	3.2g
PROTEIN		38.2g	39.2g	38.0g	14.1g
CARBS		21.4g	21.4g	21.4g	25.4g
SUGAR		2.2g	2.2g	2.2g	3.2g
SODIUM		335mg	314mg	322mg	245mg
KILOJOULES		1151(cals 274)	1188(cals 283)	1151(cals 274)	802(cals 191)
GI RATING		HIGH	HIGH	HIGH	HIGH

Swedish Meatballs with Green Pepper Sauce

SERVES: 4

MEATBALLS: ¾ cup dried breadcrumbs
¾ cup skim milk
250g each of very lean pork & beef mince
½ cup onion finely diced
1 egg white
1 teaspoon allspice
1 teaspoon crushed garlic (in jar)
1 tablespoon salt-reduced chicken-style stock powder
cooking spray
SAUCE: ¼ cup brandy
2 teaspoons green peppercorns (in can)
1 teaspoon crushed garlic (in jar)
2 teaspoons salt-reduced chicken-style stock powder
2 tablespoons cornflour
1 x 375ml can evaporated light milk

Dietitian's Tip
Mince can contain up to 33% fat, mostly saturated. There is a definite link between high saturated fat foods, diabetes and heart disease. Leaner meats can contain up to 10% fat so ask your butcher for lean pork and lean beef mince or purchase the ones with the Heart Foundation tick.

DIRECTIONS

Preheat oven 180°C fan forced.

To make meatballs: In a small bowl combine breadcrumbs and milk, leave for 2 minutes. Place all the meatball ingredients including the soaked breadcrumbs into a large mixing bowl, use your hands to combine mixture well. Roll into 32 small meatballs. Place meatballs on a flat baking tray that has been generously coated with cooking spray, spray tops of balls. Bake 25 minutes or until cooked.

To make sauce: Lightly crush peppercorns. In a small non-stick saucepan that has been coated with cooking spray, cook peppercorns and garlic for 30 seconds. Add brandy and stock powder. Combine cornflour with evaporated milk, pour into pot, stir until boiling and sauce has thickened, pour over meatballs.

Nutritional Information   Ⓕ

PER SERVE			
FAT	TOTAL		7.6g
	SATURATED		3.1g
FIBRE			0.9g
PROTEIN			26.5g
CARBS			23.4g
SUGAR			10.4g
SODIUM			249mg
KILOJOULES		1215 (cals 289)	
GI RATING			LOW

Nutritional Information   Ⓕ

PER SERVE			
FAT	TOTAL		8.3g
	SATURATED		3.8g
FIBRE			0.1g
PROTEIN			26.4g
CARBS			21.8g
SUGAR			20.9g
SODIUM			440mg
KILOJOULES		1115 (cals 265)	
GI RATING			LOW

Minted Lamb Kebabs

SERVES: 6

12 bamboo skewers
MARINADE: ½ cup thick mint sauce (Fountain®)
3 tablespoons soy sauce 43% less salt
2 tablespoons no-added-salt tomato paste
1 teaspoon crushed ginger (in jar)
1 teaspoon crushed garlic (in jar)
¼ cup yellow box honey
1 teaspoon cumin
1 teaspoon dried rosemary
KEBABS: 750g raw lean lamb rump steak (boneless chump)

Dietitian's Tip
Red meat is an excellent source of vitamin B12 (cobalamin).

DIRECTIONS

Soak bamboo skewers overnight or for several hours in water before using to avoid burning. **To make marinade:** In a small mixing bowl whisk all ingredients together. **To make kebabs:** Cut lamb into large dice. Thread onto bamboo skewers then place into a large shallow plastic container (that has a lid), pour marinade over meat. Refrigerate overnight if possible or for at least 4 hours. Turn occasionally. When ready to cook remove kebabs from marinade and either BBQ or grill turning so all sides cook. Pour marinade over meat while cooking.

Potato Lasagne

SERVES: 8

1 kilo potatoes

cooking spray

2 teaspoons crushed garlic (in jar)

500g very lean beef mince

1 cup each of onion, carrots, capsicum and celery diced

1 x 420g can no-added-salt crushed tomatoes

½ cup (140g) no-added-salt tomato paste

1 x 420g can salt-reduced tomato soup

2 teaspoons salt-reduced chicken-style stock powder

2 teaspoons dried basil

pepper

WHITE SAUCE

1 tablespoon Flora Light® margarine

4 tablespoons plain flour

2 cups skim milk

2 tablespoons grated parmesan cheese

pepper

½ cup 25% reduced-fat grated tasty cheese

DIRECTIONS

Preheat oven 180°C fan forced. Peel and cut potatoes into thin slices. Microwave potatoes with a little water on HIGH for 5 minutes. Drain well.

To make meat sauce: In a large saucepan that has been coated with cooking spray, sauté garlic and mince until cooked. Add onions, carrots, capsicum, celery, cook 3 minutes stirring occasionally. Add canned tomatoes, tomato paste and soup, combine well. Add stock powder, basil and pepper to taste. Slow boil for 3 minutes. Leave to one side.

To make white sauce: In a medium size saucepan melt margarine, add flour and combine. Slowly add milk to pan using a whisk to avoid lumps. Add parmesan cheese and pepper to taste.

To assemble lasagne: In a large lasagne dish that has been coated with cooking spray, place half the potato slices over base. Spread half the mince mixture over top of potato. Repeat this process. Spread white sauce over final mince layer, sprinkle cheese on top. Cover with foil (coat foil with cooking spray to stop cheese sticking). Bake 45 minutes then remove foil and bake 30 minutes or until potato is cooked through.

VARIATION: FOR A VEGETARIAN VERSION REPLACE CHICKEN STOCK WITH VEGETABLE STOCK POWDER AND REPLACE BEEF MINCE WITH 150g (1 BOX) TVP VEGE-MINCE. TO PREPARE TVP VEGE-MINCE FOLLOW INSTRUCTIONS ON BOX AND ADD WHEN ADDING TOMATO SOUP.

Dietitian's Tip
This low fat white sauce containing cheese and milk provides additional calcium in our eating plan. We require 2 to 3 serves of dairy products a day to meet our target for calcium and help prevent oesteoporosis.

Nutritional Information   Ⓕ

PER SERVE			MINCE	VEGETARIAN
FAT	TOTAL		8.0g	3.7g
	SATURATED		3.5g	1.7g
FIBRE			3.4g	4.1g
PROTEIN			22.9g	13.0g
CARBS			29.6g	31.1g
SUGAR			11.4g	11.9g
SODIUM			258mg	336mg
KILOJOULES			1195 (cals 285)	901 (cals 215)
GI RATING			HIGH	HIGH

Lamb Pie

SERVES: 6

600g lean lamb leg steaks
250g fresh leek
cooking spray
1 teaspoon crushed garlic (in jar)
1½ cups carrots small dice
1 cup frozen peas
2 tablespoons Gravox® Lite Supreme
½ cup water
1 x 400g can no-added-salt chopped tomatoes
2 tablespoons no-added-salt tomato paste
3 tablespoons BBQ sauce
2 tablespoons fresh mint chopped
1 tablespoon salt-reduced chicken-style stock powder
1 teaspoon dried rosemary
pepper to taste
7 sheets filo pastry (Antoniou®)

DIRECTIONS

Cut lamb into small dice. Cut end off leek then cut in half lengthways, wash leek well then cut into slices. In a large non-stick frypan that has been generously coated with cooking spray, sauté lamb and garlic until meat is browned. Add carrots and cook 4 minutes. Place leeks and peas into pan and cook 2 minutes. Combine Gravox with water. Add all remaining ingredients except filo sheets to pan, stir together well. Cook for 2-3 minutes or until thickened. Leave filling to cool.

Preheat oven 180°C fan forced.

To assemble pie: Coat a 20cm pie dish with cooking spray. Fold out 7 filo pastry sheets, cut each sheet in

Dietitian's Tip
Using filo instead of traditional pastry lowers the fat and kilojoule value of the dish and provides an interesting texture. A great tip for modifying all pie recipes. Well done Annette.

half, 8 for base, 6 for top. Layer pie dish with 8 cut sheets of pastry in a rotating fashion, spray generously with cooking spray between each sheet. Pour lamb filling on top of layered pastry. With remaining sheets repeat layering process, crinkle edges together, spray with cooking spray. Cut a small slit in top of pastry. Bake 30-35 minutes. Serve immediately as pastry will soften when left. To crisp again either place back in oven or under grill.

VARIATIONS: REPLACE LAMB WITH 750g LEAN RUMP STEAK, SKINLESS CHICKEN BREAST OR 400g TOFU DICED AND ALSO REPLACE FRESH MINT WITH FRESH PARSLEY.

Nutritional Information Ⓕ

PER SERVE		LAMB	RUMP	CHICKEN	TOFU
FAT	TOTAL	3.3g	3.7g	3.4g	5.1g
	SATURATED	1.1g	1.2g	0.7g	0.1g
FIBRE		4.5g	4.5g	4.5g	4.5g
PROTEIN		28.7g	29.3g	28.5g	12.6g
CARBS		26.5g	26.5g	26.5g	29.2g
SUGAR		9.7g	9.7g	9.7g	10.3g
SODIUM		295mg	281mg	286mg	235mg
KILOJOULES		1060(cals 252)	1085(cals 258)	1060(cals 252)	828(cals 197)
GI RATING		MEDIUM	MEDIUM	MEDIUM	MEDIUM

Roast Turkey with Cranberry Sauce

SERVES: 6

1½ cups light cranberry juice no added sugar
¼ cup dried cranberries cut in half
1 teaspoon salt-reduced chicken-style stock powder
1 tablespoon fresh lemon juice
½ teaspoon Dijon mustard (in jar)
2 tablespoons cornflour
600g cooked turkey breast sliced

DIRECTIONS

In a small non-stick saucepan place all ingredients except turkey. Using a whisk blend together. Once boiled reduce to a slow boil for 3 minutes. Pour sauce over heated turkey slices.

TIP: USE EITHER ROLLED TURKEY BREAST (FOLLOW COOKING INSTRUCTIONS ON PACKAGE) OR THICK DELI SLICED COOKED TURKEY BREAST.

Nutritional Information Ⓕ

PER SERVE		
FAT	TOTAL	4.0g
	SATURATED	0.9g
FIBRE		0.4g
PROTEIN		29.5g
CARBS		9.4g
SUGAR		5.7g
SODIUM		225mg
KILOJOULES		864 (cals 206)
GI RATING		LOW

Dietitian's Tip
Studies have shown that many people who suffer from bladder infection have fewer episodes when they drink cranberry juice or extract daily.

Sandwich Fillings

Dietitian's Tip: Annette has provided a choice of two low GI breads. Nutritionally the 9 grain bread has less carbohydrate than the white low GI bread. It is recognised that many people prefer white bread & the traditional loaf is low in fibre & has a high GI. Compared to the traditional white loaf the white low GI bread provides additional benefits for people with diabetes, heart disease & weight reduction.

Teriyaki Chicken Sandwich

SERVES: 2

cooking spray
150g raw skinless chicken breast
½ teaspoon crushed garlic (in jar)
½ teaspoon crushed ginger (in jar)
½ cup onion finely diced
⅓ cup capsicum sliced
2 tablespoons Teriyaki marinade (in bottle)
4 slices 9 grain bread or white low GI bread

This sandwich is higher in sodium (salt) than is generally recommended for people with diabetes, heart disease or high blood pressure. Be sure to make this an occasional food.

DIRECTIONS

In a small non-stick frypan that has been generously coated with cooking spray, fry chicken until cooked. Remove from pan. Coat pan again with cooking spray and sauté garlic, ginger, onion and capsicum until cooked. Add Teriyaki marinade and combine with vegetables. Slice chicken then place into pan combining with vegetables and sauce. Spread mixture over 2 slices of bread then place remaining bread slices on top.

Nutritional Information ®

PER SERVE		9 GRAIN BREAD	WHITE LOW GI BREAD
FAT	TOTAL	5.7g	4.0g
	SATURATED	1.0g	1.0g
FIBRE		3.9g	3.6g
PROTEIN		27.2g	24.3g
CARBS		27.2g	41.1g
SUGAR		3.0g	4.4g
SODIUM		596mg	674mg
KILOJOULES		1280 (cals 305)	1281 (cals 305)
GI RATING		LOW	LOW

Thai Chicken Salad Sandwich

SERVES: 2

150g raw skinless chicken breast
1 teaspoon Thai seasoning
cooking spray
4 teaspoons 97% fat-free mayonnaise
1 teaspoon soy sauce 43% less salt
1 teaspoon Thai chilli stir fry paste
4 slices 9 grain bread or white low GI bread
1 small tomato sliced
6 snow peas thinly sliced
1 tablespoon shallots sliced
½ cup bean shoots

This recipe is higher in sodium (salt) compared with other recipes in this book. People with diabetes, heart disease and high blood pressure are advised to only have this sandwich occasionally.

DIRECTIONS

Coat chicken with Thai seasoning. In a small non-stick frypan that has been generously coated with cooking spray fry chicken until cooked. Slice chicken. In a small mixing bowl combine mayonnaise with soy sauce and chilli paste then spread over 2 slices of bread. Top with salad ingredients and chicken. Place remaining bread on top.

Nutritional Information ®

PER SERVE		9 GRAIN BREAD	WHITE LOW GI BREAD
FAT	TOTAL	6.2g	4.6g
	SATURATED	1.1g	1.1g
FIBRE		4.7g	4.4g
PROTEIN		27.8g	24.9g
CARBS		25.0g	38.9g
SUGAR		6.8g	7.6g
SODIUM		554mg	631mg
KILOJOULES		1277 (cals 304)	1278 (cals 304)
GI RATING		LOW	LOW

Turkey Cranberry Sandwich

SERVES: 2

4 teaspoons cranberry sauce (in jar)
4 teaspoons Light Philadelphia® cream cheese
4 slices 9 grain bread or white low GI bread
60g deli roast turkey slices
1 cup lettuce shredded

Light Philadelphia® cream cheese has a creamy flavour and smooth texture. It has 80% less fat than butter or margarine making it an ideal lower fat choice for people wanting to lose weight.

DIRECTIONS

In a small mixing bowl mix cranberry sauce with cream cheese until combined. Spread over 2 slices of bread then top with turkey and lettuce. Place remaining bread on top.

Nutritional Information ®

PER SERVE		9 GRAIN BREAD	WHITE LOW GI BREAD
FAT	TOTAL	7.2g	5.5g
	SATURATED	0.9g	0.9g
FIBRE		3.5g	3.2g
PROTEIN		18.8g	15.9g
CARBS		24.2g	38.2g
SUGAR		6.5g	7.9g
SODIUM		348mg	425mg
KILOJOULES		1143 (cals 272)	1143 (cals 272)
GI RATING		LOW	LOW

Tuna Salad Sandwich

SERVES: 2

1 x 180g can tuna in spring water drained
¼ cup celery sliced
1½ tablespoons shallots sliced
pepper to taste
2½ tablespoons 97% fat-free mayonnaise
4 slices 9 grain bread or white low GI bread

Celery is low in kilojoules and because of its high water content (95%) celery has a crisp and crunchy texture. Some phytochemicals in celery have been reported to offer possible relief from arthritis.

DIRECTIONS

In a small mixing bowl combine tuna with celery, shallots, pepper and mayonnaise. Spread mix over 2 slices of bread then place remaining bread slices on top.

Nutritional Information ®

PER SERVE		9 GRAIN BREAD	WHITE LOW GI BREAD
FAT	TOTAL	6.5g	4.8g
	SATURATED	1.4g	1.4g
FIBRE		3.6g	3.3g
PROTEIN		29.0g	26.1g
CARBS		24.3g	38.2g
SUGAR		5.8g	7.2g
SODIUM		467mg	545mg
KILOJOULES		1294 (cals 308)	1294 (cals 308)
GI RATING		LOW	LOW

Roast Beef with Chutney Sandwich

SERVES: 2

cooking spray
½ cup onion sliced
½ cup mushrooms sliced
¼ cup fruit chutney
(in jar)
4 slices 9 grain bread or white low GI bread
60g sliced deli roast beef

DIRECTIONS

In a small non-stick frypan that has been generously coated with cooking spray, sauté onion and mushrooms until cooked. Add chutney and combine well. Spread mixture over 2 slices of bread then top with beef. Place remaining bread slices on top.

Cooking spray applied to a non-stick frypan is an excellent way to decrease your fat intake but still allows the flavours to develop from the cooked mushrooms, onions and tomatoes. A sandwich everyone will love.

Nutritional Information

PER SERVE		9 GRAIN BREAD	WHITE LOW GI BREAD
FAT	TOTAL	4.4g	2.8g
	SATURATED	0.8g	0.8g
FIBRE		4.1g	3.8g
PROTEIN		15.8g	12.9g
CARBS		32.2g	46.2g
SUGAR		14.0g	15.4g
SODIUM		551mg	628mg
KILOJOULES		1130 (cals 269)	1130 (cals 269)
GI RATING		LOW	LOW

Chicken Waldorf Sandwich

SERVES: 2

cooking spray
150g raw skinless chicken breast
⅓ cup fresh apple diced
⅓ cup celery sliced
1 tablespoon walnuts chopped
1 tablespoon onion diced
2 tablespoons 97% fat-free mayonnaise
4 slices 9 grain bread or white low GI bread
1 cup lettuce shredded

DIRECTIONS

In a small non-stick frypan that has been generously coated with cooking spray, fry chicken until cooked. Cut into small dice then place into a small mixing bowl with diced apple, celery, walnuts, onion and mayonnaise. Combine well. Spread mixture over 2 slices of bread then top with lettuce and remaining bread.

Walnuts are rich in polyunsaturated fats, omega oils and vitamins. Australian research recommends that people with diabetes eat a handful of walnuts a day to decrease the incidence of heart disease.

Nutritional Information

PER SERVE		9 GRAIN BREAD	WHITE LOW GI BREAD
FAT	TOTAL	8.8g	7.2g
	SATURATED	1.2g	1.2g
FIBRE		4.6g	4.3g
PROTEIN		26.9g	24.0g
CARBS		26.1g	40.0g
SUGAR		7.5g	8.9g
SODIUM		420mg	498mg
KILOJOULES		1375 (cals 327)	1376 (cals 328)
GI RATING		LOW	LOW

Vegetarian Sandwich

SERVES: 2

cooking spray
3 slices (54g) Vege Delight rasher bacon style diced
2 tablespoons low fat hommus
4 slices 9 grain bread or white low GI bread
1 small tomato sliced
8 slices cucumber
¼ small capsicum sliced
¼ cup carrot grated
8 small canned beetroot slices
1 cup lettuce sliced

DIRECTIONS

In a small non-stick frypan that has been generously coated with cooking spray, fry vege rashers until browned. Spread hommus over 2 slices of bread then top with bacon and salad. Place remaining bread slices on top.

Vege delight rasher bacon style provides a delicious protein rich, meat free, alternative that everyone will enjoy. Only use the amount specified in the recipe as it is high in sodium (salt), similar to "real" bacon.

Nutritional Information

PER SERVE		9 GRAIN BREAD	WHITE LOW GI BREAD
FAT	TOTAL	8.9g	7.3g
	SATURATED	1.0g	1.0g
FIBRE		5.7g	5.4g
PROTEIN		14.3g	11.4g
CARBS		24.5g	38.4g
SUGAR		3.8g	5.2g
SODIUM		498mg	576mg
KILOJOULES		1150 (cals 274)	1150 (cals 274)
GI RATING		LOW	LOW

Chilli Beef Salad Sandwich

SERVES: 2

2 teaspoons sweet chilli sauce
1 tablespoon shallots sliced
1 tablespoon 97% fat-free mayonnaise
4 slices 9 grain bread or white low GI bread
60g sliced deli roast beef
¼ cup capsicum sliced
¼ cup carrot grated
1 small tomato sliced
1 cup lettuce shredded

DIRECTIONS

In a small mixing bowl combine sweet chilli sauce and shallots with mayonnaise then spread on 2 slices of bread. Top with sliced beef and salad. Place remaining bread slices on top.

This sandwich is packed with salad and includes beef, a protein food. Beef in your lunch will increase your iron intake for the day and help you feel fuller for a longer time than salad alone.

Nutritional Information

PER SERVE		9 GRAIN BREAD	WHITE LOW GI BREAD
FAT	TOTAL	4.6g	3.0g
	SATURATED	0.8g	0.8g
FIBRE		4.6g	4.3g
PROTEIN		15.3g	12.4g
CARBS		26.1g	40.0g
SUGAR		5.3g	6.7g
SODIUM		595mg	673mg
KILOJOULES		1026 (cals 244)	1027 (cals 244)
GI RATING		LOW	LOW

Smoked Salmon Sandwich

SERVES: 2

- **100g sliced smoked salmon**
- **2 tablespoons Light Philadelphia® cream cheese**
- **12 capers chopped**
- **2 tablespoons salad onion finely diced**
- **¼ cup cucumber small dice**
- **4 slices 9 grain bread or white low GI bread**
- **1 cup lettuce shredded**

This is a great luncheon meal bound to impress your weight conscious guests. It contains some protein and omega fats and has loads of vitamins and minerals from the salad.

DIRECTIONS

Cut salmon into small pieces. In a small mixing bowl combine salmon with cream cheese, capers, onion and cucumber, mix well. Place mixture onto 2 slices of bread, top with lettuce and remaining bread slices.

Nutritional Information

PER SERVE		9 GRAIN BREAD	WHITE LOW GI BREAD
FAT	TOTAL	6.6g	5.7g
	SATURATED	1.1g	1.1g
FIBRE		2.0g	1.8g
PROTEIN		5.6g	4.2g
CARBS		10.5g	17.5g
SUGAR		1.5g	2.2g
SODIUM		371mg	410mg
KILOJOULES		677 (cals 161)	677 (cals 161)
GI RATING		LOW	LOW

Mango Chicken Curry Sandwich

SERVES: 2

- **½ frozen (65g) mango cheek**
- **cooking spray**
- **150g raw skinless chicken breast**
- **1 tablespoon 97% fat-free mayonnaise**
- **½ teaspoon red curry paste**
- **½ teaspoon soy sauce 43% low salt**
- **¼ teaspoon salt-reduced chicken-style stock powder**
- **1 tablespoon shallots sliced**
- **4 slices 9 grain bread or white low GI bread**

A totally low GI recipe that includes many water soluble vitamins, minerals and fibre. Have this sandwich with low fat yoghurt or a fruit for a complete meal suitable for people with diabetes.

DIRECTIONS

Defrost mango. In a small non-stick frypan that has been generously coated with cooking spray, fry chicken until cooked. Cut into slices. In a small mixing bowl combine mayonnaise, curry paste, soy sauce, stock powder, shallots and mango. Combine chicken with mixture, spread over 2 slices of bread. Place remaining bread slices on top.

Nutritional Information

PER SERVE		9 GRAIN BREAD	WHITE LOW GI BREAD
FAT	TOTAL	5.9g	4.2g
	SATURATED	1.1g	1.1g
FIBRE		3.8g	3.5g
PROTEIN		26.5g	23.6g
CARBS		25.5g	39.5g
SUGAR		7.3g	8.7g
SODIUM		392mg	470mg
KILOJOULES		1250 (cals 298)	1250 (cals 298)
GI RATING		LOW	LOW

Satay Chicken Sandwich

SERVES: 2

- **cooking spray**
- **150g raw skinless chicken breast**
- **1 tablespoon peanut butter**
- **½ teaspoon soy sauce 43% low salt**
- **4 teaspoons 97% fat-free mayonnaise**
- **4 slices 9 grain bread or white low GI bread**
- **⅓ cup carrot grated**
- **1 cup lettuce shredded**

Skinless chicken breast is extremely lean meat providing protein without fat. The peanut butter adds some fat - including omega fats ideal for heart health. This is a great combination of ingredients.

DIRECTIONS

In a small non-stick frypan that has been generously coated with cooking spray, fry chicken until cooked, cut into slices. In a small mixing bowl combine peanut butter, soy sauce and mayonnaise together then spread over 2 slices of bread. Top with chicken, carrot and lettuce. Place remaining bread slices on top.

Nutritional Information

PER SERVE		9 GRAIN BREAD	WHITE LOW GI BREAD
FAT	TOTAL	9.8g	8.2g
	SATURATED	1.9g	1.9g
FIBRE		4.0g	3.7g
PROTEIN		28.1g	25.2g
CARBS		22.8g	36.7g
SUGAR		4.7g	6.1g
SODIUM		465mg	543mg
KILOJOULES		1399 (cals 333)	1400 (cals 333)
GI RATING		LOW	LOW

Moroccan Chicken Sandwich

SERVES: 2

- **150g raw skinless chicken breast**
- **2 teaspoons Moroccan seasoning**
- **cooking spray**
- **4 tablespoons low-fat hommus**
- **4 slices 9 grain bread or white low GI bread**
- **⅓ cup tabouli (pre-made from supermarket)**

DIRECTIONS

Coat raw chicken with seasoning. In a small non-stick frypan that has been generously coated with cooking spray, fry chicken until cooked. Slice chicken. Spread hommus over 2 slices of bread, top with tabouli and chicken then remaining slices of bread.

Parsley is a nutritious herb containing high amounts of vitamin A and C, potassium, calcium, magnesium, phosphorus, iron and other essential minerals making it ideal to include in a healthy eating plan.

Nutritional Information

PER SERVE		9 GRAIN BREAD	WHITE LOW GI BREAD
FAT	TOTAL	8.9g	7.3g
	SATURATED	1.4g	1.4g
FIBRE		5.1g	4.8g
PROTEIN		28.6g	25.7g
CARBS		26.3g	40.2g
SUGAR		4.1g	5.5g
SODIUM		518mg	595mg
KILOJOULES		1420 (cals 338)	1421 (cals 338)
GI RATING		LOW	LOW

Philly and Fruit Sandwich

SERVES: 2

2 tablespoons Light Philadelphia® cream cheese

½ cup dried fruit medley

4 slices 9 grain bread or white low GI bread

DIRECTIONS

In a small mixing bowl combine cream cheese with dried fruit. Spread mixture over 2 slices of bread then top with remaining bread slices.

The amount of carbohydrate in this sandwich made with the white low GI bread is more than is usual for most sandwiches. Due to this many people with diabetes may choose this sandwich alone as their entire lunch meal rather than having a serve of low fat yoghurt or fruit as well.

Nutritional Information

PER SERVE		9 GRAIN BREAD	WHITE LOW GI BREAD
FAT	TOTAL	7.1g	5.5g
	SATURATED	0.6g	0.6g
FIBRE		5.6g	5.3g
PROTEIN		11.2g	8.3g
CARBS		38.6g	52.5g
SUGAR		19.7g	21.1g
SODIUM		305mg	383mg
KILOJOULES		1245 (cals 296)	1246 (cals 296)
GI RATING		LOW	LOW

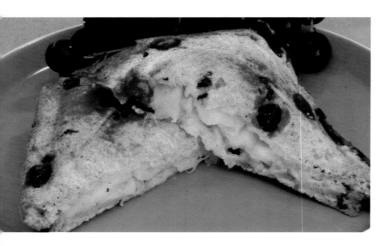

Apple Fruit Bread Jaffle

SERVES: 2

½ x 400g can pie apple

4 slices fruit bread

cooking spray

DIRECTIONS

Spoon apple mixture over 2 slices of bread then top with remaining slices. Place in a heated jaffle iron that has been coated with cooking spray until browned to your liking.

Dietitian's Tip
This recipe will provide you with fibre and loads of low GI carbohydrates. This may make you feel fuller for longer and is ideal for people following weight loss eating plans.

Nutritional Information

PER SERVE		
FAT	TOTAL	2.3g
	SATURATED	0.4g
FIBRE		3.3g
PROTEIN		4.8g
CARBS		44.1g
SUGAR		19.5g
SODIUM		145mg
KILOJOULES		897 (cals 214)
GI RATING		LOW

Sloppy Joe Jaffle

SERVES: 2

cooking spray

125g very lean beef mince

½ teaspoon crushed garlic (in jar)

¼ cup onion finely diced

½ cup fresh tomatoes diced

2 tablespoons no-added-salt tomato paste

1 teaspoon salt-reduced chicken-style stock powder

¼ teaspoon dried oregano leaves

4 slices 9 grain bread or white low GI bread

Dietitian's Tip
Research suggests that protein and high fibre low GI carbohydrate make you feel fuller for longer than other meals. Therefore this jaffle is ideal for people wanting to lose weight.

DIRECTIONS

In a small non-stick frypan that has been generously coated with cooking spray, sauté mince with garlic until cooked. Add onion and tomatoes, cook 2 minutes. Stir in tomato paste, stock powder and oregano, combine well. Spread mixture over 2 slices of bread, place remaining bread slices on top. Cook in a heated jaffle iron that has been coated with cooking spray until browned to your liking.

VARIATION: TO MAKE THE TRADITIONAL AMERICAN WAY SERVE IN A BREAD ROLL - 2 MEDIUM SIZE MULTI GRAIN BREAD ROLLS AND DIVIDE MIXTURE INTO EACH ROLL.

Nutritional Information

PER SERVE		9 GRAIN BREAD	WHITE LOW GI BREAD	M/G ROLL
FAT	TOTAL	8.3g	6.7g	6.5g
	SATURATED	2.4g	2.4g	2.1g
FIBRE		4.1g	3.8g	3.9g
PROTEIN		23.0g	20.1g	19.0g
CARBS		22.6g	36.5g	28.6g
SUGAR		4.7g	4.7g	5.1g
SODIUM		303mg	380mg	341mg
KILOJOULES		1238 (cals 295)	1238 (cals 295)	1054 (cals 251)
GI RATING		LOW	LOW	MEDIUM

Pizza Jaffle

SERVES: 2

30g lean ham diced
½ cup 25% reduced-fat grated tasty cheese
⅓ cup capsicum diced
¼ cup fresh tomatoes diced
½ cup mushrooms sliced
¼ cup onion finely diced
¼ teaspoon dried basil
½ teaspoon crushed garlic (in jar)
2 teaspoons no-added-salt tomato paste
4 slices 9 grain bread or white low GI bread
cooking spray

DIRECTIONS

In a medium size mixing bowl combine all ingredients except tomato paste and bread. Spread tomato paste over 2 slices of bread then top with pizza filling. Place remaining slices of bread on top. Cook in a heated jaffle iron that has been coated with cooking spray until browned to your liking.

Dietitian's Tip
Annette has provided us with another low fat traditional food alternative. This time a fat reduced pizza that is also moderate in sodium (salt).

Chicken Parmigiana Jaffle

SERVES: 2

cooking spray
120g raw skinless chicken breast
1½ teaspoons no-added-salt tomato paste
4 slices 9 grain bread or white low GI bread
2 slices Bega® Super Slim cheese
30g lean ham sliced

DIRECTIONS

In a small non-stick frypan that has been generously coated with cooking spray, fry chicken until cooked. Cut chicken into slices. Spread tomato paste over 2 slices of bread. Top with chicken, cheese and ham. Place remaining bread slices on top. Place in a heated jaffle iron that has been coated with cooking spray until browned to your liking.

Dietitian's Tip
Annette has cleverly used reduced fat cheese, lean meat and cooking spray to fry the chicken. The result is a delicious chicken parmigiana - without the fat and suitable for people with diabetes.

Tuna and Corn Jaffle

SERVES: 2

1 x 180g can tuna in spring water
½ cup (125g can) creamed corn
1 tablespoon shallots sliced
pepper
4 slices 9 grain bread or white low GI bread
cooking spray

DIRECTIONS

In a small mixing bowl combine drained tuna with creamed corn, shallots and pepper to taste. Spread mixture over 2 slices of bread then place remaining bread slices on top. Cook in a heated jaffle iron that has been coated with cooking spray until browned to your liking.

Nutritional Information:	Pizza Jaffle		Chicken Parmigiana Jaffle		Tuna and Corn Jaffle	
PER SERVE	**9 GRAIN BREAD**	**WHITE LOW GI BREAD**	**9 GRAIN BREAD**	**WHITE LOW GI BREAD**	**9 GRAIN BREAD**	**WHITE LOW GI BREAD**
FAT TOTAL	9.1g	7.5g	7.7g	6.1g	6.4g	4.7g
SATURATED	3.8g	3.8g	2.4g	2.4g	1.5g	1.4g
FIBRE	4.0g	3.7g	3.3g	3.0g	5.4g	5.1g
PROTEIN	18.2g	15.3g	30.2g	27.3g	30.1g	27.2g
CARBS	21.9g	35.9g	20.7g	34.6g	29.8g	43.7g
SUGAR	3.6g	5.0g	2.4g	4.1g	4.9g	6.3g
SODIUM	481mg	559mg	503mg	581mg	510mg	588mg
KILOJOULES	1173 (cals 279)	1174 (cals 279)	1303 (cals 310)	1304 (cals 310)	1402 (cals 334)	1403 (cals 334)
GI RATING	LOW	LOW	LOW	LOW	LOW	LOW

Caesar Toasted Sandwich

SERVES: 2

cooking spray

30g 97% fat-free bacon short cuts diced

1 boiled egg chopped

1½ teaspoons grated parmesan cheese

4 teaspoons 99% fat-free Caesar dressing

1 cup lettuce shredded

4 slices 9 grain bread or white low GI bread

DIRECTIONS

In a small non-stick frypan that has been coated with cooking spray, fry bacon until browned. Place all the ingredients into a small mixing bowl, except bread, combine well. Toast bread slices. Place mixture onto 2 slices of toast then top with remaining toast slices.

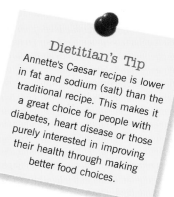

Dietitian's Tip
Annette's Caesar recipe is lower in fat and sodium (salt) than the traditional recipe. This makes it a great choice for people with diabetes, heart disease or those purely interested in improving their health through making better food choices.

Grilled Vegetable Toasted Sandwich

SERVES: 2

140g pumpkin

1 medium size zucchini

1 medium size capsicum

¼ cup onion sliced

cooking spray

4 slices 9 grain bread or white low GI bread

2 teaspoons pesto (in jar)

DIRECTIONS

Cut pumpkin into thin slices. Slice zucchini length ways into thin slices. Cut capsicum in half, de-core and remove seeds. Place all vegetables on a flat baking tray that has been generously coated with cooking spray, spray over top of vegetables and place under hot griller until browned turning once. Peel skin off capsicum. Toast bread until browned then spread pesto over 2 slices. Top with vegetables and remaining toast. Serve hot or cold.

Dietitian's Tip
Grilled vegetables can be eaten hot or cold and will tempt even the fussiest of eaters. If you are having trouble making your 5 veggies a day try including grilled vegetables in your eating plan. Capsicum is particularly high in vitamin C.

Nutritional Information ®

PER SERVE		9 GRAIN BREAD	WHITE LOW GI BREAD
FAT	TOTAL	7.6g	6.0g
	SATURATED	2.0g	2.0g
FIBRE		3.6g	3.3g
PROTEIN		15.7g	12.8g
CARBS		21.5g	35.4g
SUGAR		3.3g	4.7g
SODIUM		548mg	626mg
KILOJOULES		1063 (cals 253)	1064 (cals 253)
GI RATING		LOW	LOW

Nutritional Information ®

PER SERVE		9 GRAIN BREAD	WHITE LOW GI BREAD
FAT	TOTAL	6.4g	4.8g
	SATURATED	1.2g	1.2g
FIBRE		6.3g	6.0g
PROTEIN		13.0g	10.1g
CARBS		27.4g	41.3g
SUGAR		7.9g	9.3g
SODIUM		299mg	377mg
KILOJOULES		1071 (cals 255)	1072 (cals 255)
GI RATING		LOW	LOW

Alaskan Crab Open Grill Sandwich

SERVES: 6 SLICES

6 slices 9 grain bread or white low GI bread

1 tablespoon Flora Light® margarine

¼ cup shallots sliced

2 tablespoons dry white wine

2 teaspoons fresh parsley chopped

1 x 170g can crab meat drained

1 tablespoon cornflour

¼ cup skim milk

pepper to taste

½ cup 25% reduced-fat grated tasty cheese

DIRECTIONS

Toast bread. In a medium size saucepan melt margarine, sauté shallots for 30 seconds. Add wine and cook for 15 seconds. Add parsley and crab meat. Blend cornflour with milk, pour into pan stirring continuously until boiling and thickened, add pepper. Spread a sixth of the mixture over each slice of toasted bread. Sprinkle cheese on top, place under griller until cheese has melted and browned. Cut each slice into three fingers.

Dietitian's Tip
Crab is an excellent source of protein and is low in fat. A meal with crab, low GI bread and lots of salad goes a long way to providing your daily requirements of vitamins and minerals.

Nutritional Information

PER SLICE		9 GRAIN BREAD	WHITE LOW GI BREAD
FAT	TOTAL	3.9g	3.1g
	SATURATED	1.6g	1.6g
FIBRE		1.7g	1.6g
PROTEIN		10.3g	8.9g
CARBS		11.9g	18.8g
SUGAR		1.5g	2.2g
SODIUM		302mg	341mg
KILOJOULES		615 (cals 146)	615 (cals 146)
GI RATING		LOW	LOW

Bruschetta

SERVES: 4

3 medium size (400g) ripe tomatoes

¼ small salad onion finely diced

2 small cloves fresh garlic finely chopped

1½ tablespoons fresh basil finely chopped

1 teaspoon salt-reduced vegetable stock powder

2 teaspoons virgin olive oil

pepper to taste

1 x 170g French bread stick

DIRECTIONS

Score or cut a small cross at the bottom of each tomato. Drop tomatoes into a large saucepan that is three quarters filled with boiling water and boil for 1 minute. Remove and cool under cold water, peel skin from tomatoes. Cut tomatoes in half then using your hands squeeze as much juice out as possible (juice is not needed). Chop tomato flesh then place into a large mixing bowl. Add all other ingredients except bread into the bowl and combine well. Cut bread stick in half then cut each piece in half length ways giving you four pieces. Toast bread under griller then top with tomato filling. Serve cold or place under griller for a few minutes to heat through.

Dietitian's Tip
Bruschetta is an ideal appetiser. The dish is simple to make, highly nutritious and tastes great. Your health conscious guests will love it.

Nutritional Information

PER SERVE		
FAT	TOTAL	4.0g
	SATURATED	0.5g
FIBRE		3.1g
PROTEIN		5.0g
CARBS		25.1g
SUGAR		4.0g
SODIUM		252mg
KILOJOULES		663 (cals 158)
GI RATING		HIGH

Desserts

Mango Passionfruit Cheesecake

Mango Passionfruit Cheesecake

SERVES: 12

BASE: 15 Highland oatmeal biscuits

1 tablespoon (15g) Flora Light® margarine melted

2 teaspoons skim milk

cooking spray

FILLING: 1 x 500g tub low-fat cottage cheese

125g Light Philadelphia® cream cheese

⅓ cup sugar

300g frozen mango cheeks defrosted

2 x 200g tubs diet mango yoghurt

1 sachet mango flavoured lite jelly crystals

1½ tablespoons gelatine

⅓ cup boiling water

⅓ cup passionfruit pulp (about 3-4)

DIRECTIONS

To make base: In a food processor crush biscuits. Add melted margarine and milk, blend together. Coat a 22cm spring-form cake tin with cooking spray, press biscuit mix evenly over base. Refrigerate.

To make filling: Clean food processor. Blend cottage cheese until very smooth, add cream cheese and combine well. Slowly pour in sugar, mix until dissolved. Add defrosted mango and mix until combined. Pour mixture into a large mixing bowl. Add yoghurt and combine using an electric beater. Dissolve jelly crystals and gelatine in boiling water then pour into mixture, beat well. Pour filling over biscuit base. Refrigerate. Once set spread passionfruit pulp evenly over top of cheesecake.

VARIATION: REPLACE FROZEN MANGO CHEEKS WITH 800g CANNED MANGO SLICES DRAINED.

Dietitian's Tip
Annette has developed a very clever dessert that is low in fat. This is one of my favourite healthy dessert recipes.

Pear and Almond Tart

SERVES: 10

3 medium size fresh pears

½ cup brown sugar

cooking spray

1 egg white

3 tablespoons white sugar

2 tablespoons (30g) Flora Light® margarine melted

2 tablespoons skim milk

⅓ cup ground almonds (almond meal)

½ teaspoon imitation almond essence

½ cup self-raising flour

½ cup cornflour

Dietitian's Tip
Almonds contain protein, carbohydrate and concentrations of calcium, phosphorus and magnesium, as well as vitamins from groups B and E. They also have high content of fat (both mono-unsaturated and polyunsaturated) and the highest fibre content of any nut or seed. Including almonds in your eating plan will decrease your risk of heart disease.

DIRECTIONS

Preheat oven 180°C fan forced.

Peel and core pears. Cut into slices. Spread brown sugar evenly over base of a quiche or pie dish that has been coated with cooking spray. Place layers of pear slices in a circular fashion over sugared base. In a medium size mixing bowl beat egg white and white sugar using an electric beater for 30 seconds. Add melted margarine, milk, ground almonds, essence and combine. Place sifted flours into bowl, fold until combined, if needed use your hands to work the mixture. Roll out pastry onto a well floured surface to the shape and size of dish. Place rolled pastry on top of pear. Bake 30 minutes. Gently turn tart upside down onto serving plate. Serve either hot or cold.

VARIATION: REPLACE PEARS WITH FRESH GREEN APPLES.

Nutritional Information Ⓕ

PER SERVE		
FAT	TOTAL	4.9g
	SATURATED	0.6g
FIBRE		1.6g
PROTEIN		11.6g
CARBS		15.9g
SUGAR		13.6g
SODIUM		166mg
KILOJOULES	649 (cals 155)	
GI RATING		LOW

Nutritional Information Ⓕ

PER SERVE		
FAT	TOTAL	3.6g
	SATURATED	0.4g
FIBRE		1.7g
PROTEIN		2.0g
CARBS		27.6g
SUGAR		15.5g
SODIUM		70mg
KILOJOULES	623 (cals 148)	
GI RATING		MEDIUM

Chocolate Berry Profiteroles

SERVES: 6

PROFITEROLES

2 tablespoons (30g) Flora Light® margarine

½ cup boiling water

1 teaspoon sugar

½ cup plain flour

1 egg white

1 whole egg

cooking spray

Dietitian's Tip
A lower fat alternative to traditional profiteroles. Your family will enjoy these on special occasions.

CUSTARD

¾ cup skim milk

1½ tablespoons custard powder

1½ tablespoons sugar

¼ teaspoon vanilla essence

¾ cup frozen mixed berries

CHOCOLATE SAUCE

8 squares (32g) dark cooking chocolate

⅓ cup skim milk

¾ teaspoon cornflour

DIRECTIONS

Preheat oven 210°C fan forced

To make profiteroles: In a medium size saucepan combine margarine, water and sugar. Bring to boil, stir occasionally. Add flour in one go, stir vigorously with wooden spoon until mixture comes completely together and forms a ball. Remove and place in a medium size mixing bowl, allow to cool for 2 minutes. In a small mixing bowl beat egg white and whole egg together using a fork. Slowly beat the eggs into mixture using an electric beater until it forms a smooth shiny dough. Coat a baking tray with cooking spray then spoon a dessertspoon of mixture onto tray. Makes 12 balls. Bake 10 minutes on 210°C then reduce oven to 180°C for 20 minutes or until balls are golden brown. Leave to cool.

To make custard: Place all custard ingredients except berries into a small saucepan, stir continuously using a whisk until custard boils. Leave to cool. Fold berries gently through custard.

To make chocolate sauce: Place all chocolate sauce ingredients into a small saucepan. Cook on a slow heat until mixture boils. Simmer for 1 minute, stir continuously. Leave to cool.

To prepare chocolate profiteroles: Once all ingredients have cooled, cut balls in half using a sharp knife. Spoon custard filling into the bottom half of each ball, then top with other half. Spoon an even amount of chocolate sauce over each one. Refrigerate.

VARIATION: FOR A QUICK CHOCOLATE TOPPING REPLACE CHOCOLATE SAUCE WITH 6 TEASPOONS NUTELLA (ONE HALF TEASPOON PER BALL).

Nutritional Information (F)

PER SERVE		CHOCOLATE	NUTELLA
FAT	TOTAL	5.2g	5.1g
	SATURATED	2.3g	1.3g
FIBRE		1.5g	1.3g
PROTEIN		5.0g	5.1g
CARBS		19.1g	17.8g
SUGAR		8.6g	7.7g
SODIUM		63mg	56mg
KILOJOULES		598 (cals 142)	567 (cals 135)
GI RATING		MEDIUM	MEDIUM

Stuffed Baked Apples

MAKES: 6 APPLES

6 x 125g granny smith apples

¼ cup sultanas

¼ cup dried apricots chopped

¼ cup seedless prunes chopped

DIRECTIONS

Preheat oven 180°C fan forced.

Remove core keeping apple whole. Combine all dried fruit, stuff into apples. Using a small knife lightly score a circle through the skin around the centre of each apple (this will stop skin bursting). Place apples upright in a baking dish that is a quarter filled with water. Bake 45-50 minutes or until apples are cooked.

Nutritional Information (F)

PER APPLE		
FAT	TOTAL	0.2g
	SATURATED	0g
FIBRE		4.4g
PROTEIN		1.1g
CARBS		28.7g
SUGAR		26.6g
SODIUM		7mg
KILOJOULES		495 (cals 138)
GI RATING		LOW

Pumpkin Pie

SERVES: 12

PASTRY: ¼ cup self-raising flour
¾ cup plain flour
2 tablespoons sugar
2 tablespoons (30g) Flora
Light® margarine melted
1 tablespoon skim milk
1 egg white
cooking spray
FILLING: 3 cups (450g)
raw pumpkin small dice
2 whole eggs
2 egg whites
½ cup sugar
1 teaspoon each of cinnamon and nutmeg
1½ cups skim milk

Dietitian's Tip
Pumpkin is a good source of many vitamins and minerals. Australian dietary recommendations suggest 5 serves of veggies a day to achieve good health.

DIRECTIONS

Preheat oven 180°C fan forced. **To make pastry:** In a medium size mixing bowl combine flours and sugar together. Add melted margarine to milk, beat in egg white with a fork, pour into flour. Fold together, if needed use your hands to help blend ingredients. Place onto a well floured surface and roll out to fit a 23cm pie dish that has been coated with cooking spray. Roll up pastry using a rolling pin, lift into pie plate. Trim around edges. **To make filling:** Microwave pumpkin with a little water on HIGH for 10 minutes or until pumpkin is cooked. Drain and mash (should equal 1½ cups). In a large mixing bowl beat eggs and egg whites together with sugar for 1 minute using an electric beater. Add pumpkin, cinnamon, nutmeg and milk mixing until well combined. Pour over pastry and bake 1 hour 15 minutes. Leave to cool.

Baked Fruit Salad Cheesecake

SERVES: 12

BASE
12 Highland oatmeal biscuits
2 teaspoons skim milk
cooking spray
FILLING
1 x 250g tub low-fat cottage cheese
1 x 220g tub Philadelphia® extra light cream cheese
1 cup canned light condensed milk
1 x 440g can traditional fruit salad in natural juice

Dietitian's Tip
This low fat cheesecake with less than 3g of fat per serve is a fantastic dessert option for people with diabetes. Traditional cheesecakes can contain over 15g of fat per serve, much of which will be saturated fat.

DIRECTIONS

Preheat oven 150°C fan forced.

To make base: In a food processor crush biscuits, add milk and blend together. Coat a 23cm pie plate with cooking spray and press biscuit mix onto base. Refrigerate.

To make filling: Clean food processor. Beat cottage cheese until very smooth, add cream cheese and blend well. Pour in condensed milk and combine well. Pour mixture into a large mixing bowl, fold fruit salad including juice into mixture. Pour over biscuit base. Bake 30 minutes or until firm to touch in centre. Leave to cool then refrigerate.

VARIATION: REPLACE FRUIT SALAD WITH CANNED CRUSHED PINEAPPLE IN NATURAL JUICE.

Nutritional Information Ⓕ

PER SERVE

FAT	TOTAL	2.4g
	SATURATED	0.7g
FIBRE		0.9g
PROTEIN		5.2g
CARBS		20.8g
SUGAR		11.4g
SODIUM		70mg
KILOJOULES		521 (cals 124)
GI RATING		MEDIUM

Nutritional Information Ⓕ

PER SERVE

FAT	TOTAL	2.7g
	SATURATED	0.8g
FIBRE		0.6g
PROTEIN		8.2g
CARBS		25.8g
SUGAR		24.3g
SODIUM		174mg
KILOJOULES		668 (cals 159)
GI RATING		MEDIUM

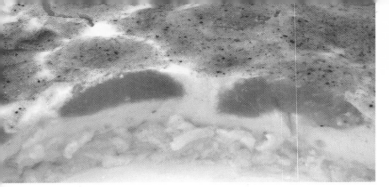

Apricot Rice Baked Custard

SERVES: 8

- ¼ cup raw Basmati rice
- 3 teaspoons sugar
- 1 x 400g can apricot halves in natural juice
- 2 whole eggs
- 2 egg whites
- 4 tablespoons sugar
- ¾ teaspoon vanilla essence
- 2½ cups skim milk
- nutmeg

Dietitian's Tip
Fruit added to a dessert increases the nutritional composition. Try this healthy rice pudding.

DIRECTIONS

Preheat oven 180°C fan forced. Boil rice with sugar following cooking instructions on rice packet. Rinse and drain well. Spread rice over base of an 8-10 cup casserole dish. Drain apricots then place on top of rice, flat side down. Add eggs, egg whites, sugar, essence and milk into a large mixing bowl and beat using an electric beater until well combined. Gently pour mixture over apricots. Sprinkle nutmeg on top. Place dish into a baking tray that is one third filled with water. Bake 1 hour or until firm to touch in centre. Serve hot or cold.

VARIATION: OMIT APRICOTS FOR PLAIN BAKED RICE CUSTARD.

Nutritional Information ℉

PER SERVE		APRICOT	PLAIN
FAT	TOTAL	1.4g	1.4g
	SATURATED	0.5g	0.5g
FIBRE		0.6g	0.1g
PROTEIN		6.1g	5.9g
CARBS		18.4g	15.9g
SUGAR		12.9g	10.7g
SODIUM		67mg	66mg
KILOJOULES		458 (cals 109)	410 (cals 98)
GI RATING		LOW	LOW

Crème Brulée

MAKES: 6

- 2 whole eggs
- 2 egg whites
- ¼ cup sugar
- 1 teaspoon vanilla essence
- 2 cups trim milk
- 1 cup canned evaporated light milk
- 6 tablespoons brown sugar

Dietitian's Tip
Desserts that include milk provide added calcium for strong bones and teeth.

DIRECTIONS

Preheat oven 160°C fan forced. In a large mixing bowl beat whole eggs and egg whites with sugar using an electric beater until combined. Add essence, trim and evaporated milks and beat well. Pour into 6 small (200ml) ramekin dishes. Place into a baking dish that has been one third filled with water. Bake 45 minutes. Remove from water when cooked, leave to cool. Before serving spread one tablespoon of brown sugar over top of each ramekin. Place under hot griller until sugar has melted and caramelised. Be careful not to overcook as the sugar will burn. Serve within 10 minutes as the sugar will start to dissolve.

Nutritional Information ℉

PER SERVE		
FAT	TOTAL	3.5g
	SATURATED	1.7g
FIBRE		0g
PROTEIN		10.2g
CARBS		26.2g
SUGAR		26.2g
SODIUM		123mg
KILOJOULES		728 (cals 173)
GI RATING		LOW

Berry Dream

SERVES: 8

- **2 cups frozen mixed berries**
- **¾ cup CHILLED evaporated light milk**
- **2 x 200g tubs diet berry yoghurt**
- **1 sachet lite raspberry jelly crystals**
- **¼ cup boiling water**

DIRECTIONS

Before starting make sure evaporated milk is chilled.

Semi defrost berries. Using an electric beater beat chilled evaporated milk until thick and stiff peaks form. Pour in yoghurt then add berries and beat until well combined. Dissolve jelly crystals with boiling water, pour into bowl beating until all mixture is blended (there should still be small pieces of berries through mixture). Either leave in bowl or divide into 8 dessert dishes. Refrigerate until set.

VARIATION: REPLACE BERRIES WITH ANY FROZEN BERRIES OF YOUR CHOICE.

Nutritional Information ℉

PER SERVE				
FAT	TOTAL	0.5g	SUGAR	6.4g
	SATURATED	0.2g	SODIUM	50mg
FIBRE		1.7g	KILOJOULES	251 (cals 60)
PROTEIN		4.4g	GI RATING	TOO LOW IN
CARBS		8.7g	CARBS TO SCORE A RATING

Black Forest Cake

SERVES: 14

CAKE: 2 egg whites
2 whole eggs separated
½ cup caster sugar
½ cup cornflour
¼ cup self-raising flour
¼ cup cocoa
¾ teaspoon bicarb soda
1 teaspoon baking powder
2 tablespoons custard powder
cooking spray
baking paper
FILLING: 1 x 500g tub low-fat cottage cheese
⅓ cup sugar
½ teaspoon vanilla essence
½ teaspoon gelatine
1 tablespoon boiling water
1 x 425g can stoneless black cherries
⅓ cup cherry brandy liqueur
2 tablespoons cornflour
3 small squares dark chocolate grated

Nutritional Information ⓕ

PER SERVE		
FAT	TOTAL	2.1g
	SATURATED	0.7g
FIBRE		0.6g
PROTEIN		6.7g
CARBS		29.0g
SUGAR		20.4g
SODIUM		208mg
KILOJOULES		726 (cals 173)
GI RATING		MEDIUM

DIRECTIONS

Preheat oven 180°C fan forced.

To make cake: In a large mixing bowl beat all egg whites with an electric beater until stiff peaks form. Gradually add sugar beating constantly. Beat in egg yolks on low speed. Sift cornflour, self-raising flour, cocoa, bicarb soda, baking and custard powders into bowl. Using a large spoon, gently fold together. Pour mixture into a lamington tray (31 x 25cm) that has been coated with cooking spray and layered with baking paper. Bake 15-20 minutes or until cake springs back when touched. Allow cake to sit 5 minutes in tray before turning onto a wire rack to cool, gently peel off paper.

To make filling: In a food processor beat cottage cheese until smooth. Add sugar and essence, beat until sugar has dissolved. In boiling water dissolve gelatine, add to food processor and blend well. Pour into a large mixing bowl and refrigerate. Drain cherries, reserving juice to make jelly. Cut cherries in half. In a small saucepan combine the saved juice and cornflour, using a whisk stir continuously on medium heat until boiled. Remove and leave to one side.

To assemble cake: Cut sponge in half length ways to make two pieces. Carefully cut through each piece again length ways so you have 4 layers of sponge. Place first layer onto a large flat serving plate. Place half the cherries cut side down over sponge and spoon over half the cherry brandy. Spread a third of the cream filling over the cherries evenly. Place a layer of sponge with the cut side facing up on top and spread cherry jelly over sponge. Place another layer of cake on top, spread remaining cherries over cake. Spoon cherry brandy over cherries then spread half of the cream on top. Place final layer of sponge cut side down and coat top with remaining cream. Sprinkle grated chocolate over top. Refrigerate to set.

Baking

Symple Jumbles

Symple Jumbles

MAKES: 24 BISCUITS

- 1 egg white
- ⅓ cup sugar
- ¼ cup skim milk
- 2 tablespoons honey
- ½ teaspoon vanilla essence
- 4 tablespoons (60g) Flora Light® margarine melted
- 1 teaspoon allspice
- 1 teaspoon mixed spice
- 1 teaspoon ground ginger
- 2 teaspoons cinnamon
- 1½ cups self-raising flour
- cooking spray
- ICING: 1 small freezer bag
- a little skim milk
- ½ cup icing sugar sifted
- red food colouring (optional)

DIRECTIONS

Preheat oven 180°C fan forced.

To make biscuits: In a medium size mixing bowl beat egg white and sugar for 1 minute using an electric beater. Add milk, honey and essence to melted margarine and place in bowl, combine together. Add spices and mix together then fold flour into mix. Spoon twenty four tablespoons of mixture onto flat baking trays that have been coated with cooking spray. Dip a fork into boiling water then slightly press the dough flat (this stops the dough from sticking to the fork). Bake 20-25 minutes or until golden brown. Leave to cool.

To make icing: Carefully snip a tiny part off a bottom corner of the plastic bag.

In a small mixing bowl combine enough milk with icing sugar until a slightly runny consistency. Add a few drops of colouring to mixture to give icing a pink colour (optional). Spoon into bag. Squeeze a little icing out in a squiggle fashion over each biscuit. Leave to set.

Dietitian's Tip
This delightful spicy low fat biscuit is recommended for people with diabetes on special occasions. Each biscuit has a similar carbohydrate and kilojoule value as a piece of fruit but unlike fruit it is low in vitamins and minerals.

Pikelets

MAKES: 24 PIKELETS

- 2 egg whites
- 2 tablespoons sugar
- ½ teaspoon white vinegar
- 1 cup skim milk
- 1 tablespoon (15g) Flora Light® margarine
- 1½ cups self-raising flour
- cooking spray

DIRECTIONS

In a medium size mixing bowl beat egg whites and sugar for 30 seconds using an electric beater. Add vinegar to milk (don't worry if the milk curdles). Melt margarine then pour into milk. Add to bowl and combine. Sift flour into mixture in one go and fold gently, DO NOT BEAT as this will make the pikelets tough. Coat frypan generously with cooking spray then drop spoonfuls of mixture onto hot frypan. When mixture starts bubbling turn pikelets over and cook other side for a few minutes. Repeat this step spraying with cooking spray each time until all mixture has been used.
Makes approximately 24 pikelets.

VARIATION: FOR SULTANA PIKELETS ADD ½ CUP SULTANAS TO MIX BEFORE FLOUR IS ADDED TO BOWL.

Dietitian's Tip
Add mixed berries and low fat yoghurt for a healthy dessert suitable for people with diabetes.

Nutritional Information

PER BISCUIT		
FAT	TOTAL	1.4g
	SATURATED	0.3g
FIBRE		0.3g
PROTEIN		1.2g
CARBS		13.2g
SUGAR		6.8g
SODIUM		74mg
KILOJOULES		289 (69)
GI RATING		MEDIUM

Nutritional Information

PER PIKELET		PLAIN	SULTANA
FAT	TOTAL	0.4g	0.4g
	SATURATED	0.1g	0.1g
FIBRE		0.3g	0.5g
PROTEIN		1.5g	1.6g
CARBS		7.6g	10.2g
SUGAR		1.4g	4.0g
SODIUM		72mg	74mg
KILOJOULES		170 (cals 40)	215 (cals 51)
GI RATING		TOO LOW IN CARBS TO SCORE A RATING	

Berry Nice Slice

MAKES: 15 SLICES

1 egg white

⅓ cup sugar

1 tablespoon golden syrup

4 tablespoons (60g) Flora Light® margarine melted

2 tablespoons skim milk

1 cup self-raising wholemeal flour

3 cups Light 'n' Tasty Triple Berry Cereal

¼ cup sultanas

¼ cup dried cranberries chopped

¼ cup pitted dried dates chopped

cooking spray

Dietitian's Tip
Goes great with a coffee. These are a suitable low fat alternative to commercial sweet biscuits.

DIRECTIONS

Preheat oven 180°C fan forced.

In a large mixing bowl beat egg white and sugar for 30 seconds using an electric beater until combined. Blend golden syrup to melted margarine then add to milk and combine, pour into bowl. Add flour, cereal and dried fruits and combine well. Coat a slab tin with cooking spray, press mixture evenly over base of tin. Bake 30 minutes. Once cooled cut into 15 slices.

VARIATION: REPLACE TRIPLE BERRY CEREAL WITH LIGHT 'N' TASTY APRICOT CEREAL.

Nutritional Information   Ⓡ

PER SLICE		
FAT	TOTAL	2.4g
	SATURATED	1.1g
FIBRE		2.6g
PROTEIN		2.6g
CARBS		26.2g
SUGAR		15.0g
SODIUM		117mg
KILOJOULES		574 (cals 137)
GI RATING		MEDIUM

Apple Fruit Cake

SERVES: 15

1½ cups dried mixed fruit

1 x 400g can pie apple

1 teaspoon allspice

1 teaspoon mixed spice

1 cup water

1 teaspoon bicarb soda

3 egg whites

2 cups self-raising flour

cooking spray

Dietitian's Tip
A great tasting fruit cake packed with vitamins and minerals. If you are aiming to lose weight or have diabetes refrain from going back for another serve.

DIRECTIONS

In a medium size saucepan place mixed fruit, apple, spices and water, bring to boil then slow boil for 3 minutes. Remove from heat, stir in bicarb soda, leave to cool.

Preheat oven 180°C fan forced.

When fruit mixture has cooled beat egg whites into fruit mixture well. Gently fold flour into mixture in one go. Pour mixture into a 19cm round cake tin or large loaf tin that has been generously coated with cooking spray. Bake 55-60 minutes or until firm to touch in centre. Allow cake to sit for 5 minutes in tin before turning onto a wire rack to cool.

NOTE: In humid weather this cake is best kept refrigerated.

Nutritional Information   Ⓕ

PER SERVE		
FAT	TOTAL	0.4g
	SATURATED	0.1g
FIBRE		1.9g
PROTEIN		3.0g
CARBS		27.0g
SUGAR		13.3g
SODIUM		193mg
KILOJOULES		516 (cals 123)
GI RATING		MEDIUM

Gluten Free Carrot Cake

SERVES: 12

3 egg whites
⅓ cup sugar
¾ teaspoon bicarb soda
½ cup apple sauce (in jar)
1 cup carrot grated
¼ cup each walnuts chopped and currants
1 teaspoon each of mixed spice, dried ginger
and fresh orange peel
½ cup fresh orange juice
½ cup wheat-free cornflour
½ cup soy compound blend
1 cup gluten-free self-raising flour
cooking spray
ICING: ½ cup icing sugar
2 tablespoons Light
Philadelphia® cream cheese

Dietitian's Tip
A great tasting recipe for people with diabetes and coeliac disease. Well done Annette. This cake contains loads of carbohydrate and may not be an ideal choice for people with diabetes who do not require a gluten free eating plan.

DIRECTIONS

Preheat oven 180°C fan forced. Beat egg whites and sugar together in a medium size mixing bowl for 1 minute using an electric beater. Stir bicarb soda into apple sauce (it will froth), then add to bowl. Fold in carrots, walnuts, currants, spices, peel and juice, combine well. Sift all three flours into mixture in one go, gently fold ingredients together, DO NOT BEAT as this will make the cake tough. Once flour is combined, pour into a 19cm round cake tin that has been coated with cooking spray. Bake 30-35 minutes or until cake springs back when lightly pressed in centre. Turn onto a wire rack to cool. **To make icing:** Mix icing ingredients then spread over top of cooled cake.

VARIATIONS: ICING - REPLACE CREAM CHEESE WITH 1 TEASPOON FLORA LIGHT® MARGARINE AND ENOUGH JUICE FROM A LEMON TO MAKE SPREADABLE OR FOR A LOWER FAT AND CARB COUNT OMIT ICING ALTOGETHER.

Nutritional Information   Ⓕ

PER SERVE		CR/CHEESE ICING	LEMON ICING	WITHOUT ICING
FAT	TOTAL	3.3g	3.0g	2.8g
	SATURATED	0.3g	0.3g	0.3g
FIBRE		2.6g	2.6g	2.6g
PROTEIN		8.1g	7.9g	7.9g
CARBS		32.3g	32.2g	26.5g
SUGAR		17.4g	17.3g	11.6g
SODIUM		80mg	73mg	70mg
KILOJOULES		794 (cals 189)	778 (cals 185)	678 (cals 161)
GI RATING		MEDIUM	MEDIUM	MEDIUM

Pear and Cranberry Loaf

MAKES: 12 SLICES

2 small fresh pears
2 egg whites
⅓ cup sugar
½ cup light cranberry juice
½ teaspoon bicarb soda
½ teaspoon cinnamon
½ cup dried cranberries
2 tablespoons (30g) Flora
Light® margarine melted
1¾ cups self-raising flour
cooking spray

Dietitian's Tip
A loaf full of fruit and low in fat. Great to serve to your guests who like to eat healthy, tasty foods.

DIRECTIONS

Preheat oven 180°C fan forced.

Peel and core pears, then cut into small dice. In a medium size mixing bowl beat egg whites and sugar for 1 minute using an electric beater. Add diced pears, cranberry juice, bicarb soda, cinnamon, cranberries and melted margarine. Combine well. Sift flour into bowl in one go and gently fold mixture until flour is just combined, DO NOT BEAT as this will make the loaf tough. Pour mixture into a large loaf tin that has been coated with cooking spray. Bake 30-35 minutes or until cooked in centre. Turn onto a wire rack to cool.

VARIATION: REPLACE PEAR WITH FRESH APPLE.

Nutritional Information   Ⓕ

PER SLICE		
FAT	TOTAL	1.5g
	SATURATED	0.3g
FIBRE		1.3g
PROTEIN		2.7g
CARBS		25.8g
SUGAR		10.6g
SODIUM		208mg
KILOJOULES		530 (cals 126)
GI RATING		MEDIUM

Chocolate Slice

MAKES: 15 SLICES

BASE: 1 cup self-raising flour
¼ cup cocoa
2 Weet-bix® crushed
½ cup sugar
2 tablespoons desiccated coconut
4 tablespoons (60g) Flora Light® margarine melted
2 tablespoons skim milk
1 egg white
cooking spray
ICING: ¾ cup icing sugar
1 tablespoon cocoa
1 teaspoon Flora Light® margarine
2-3 teaspoons skim milk
1½ teaspoons desiccated coconut (optional)

Dietitian's Tip
Wow, I love the taste of chocolate. This is low in fat but also low on the nutrient front. Don't go back for seconds - definitely a special occasion food.

DIRECTIONS

Preheat oven 180°C fan forced. **To make base:** Sift flour and cocoa into a large mixing bowl with crushed Weet-bix, sugar and coconut. Add melted margarine to milk. Using a fork beat egg white into milk until combined, pour into flour and fold together. Spread mixture over the base of a slab tin that has been coated with cooking spray. Use the palm of your hand to flatten and spread. You may need to dip your hand into flour to avoid mixture sticking. Bake 35 minutes. **To make icing:** Sift icing sugar and cocoa into a small mixing bowl. Add margarine and milk, blend well. Spread over slice while base is still warm. Sprinkle coconut over top, leave to cool.

Nutritional Information   Ⓕ

PER SLICE		
FAT	TOTAL	3.1g
	SATURATED	1.0g
FIBRE		0.8g
PROTEIN		1.9g
CARBS		21.2g
SUGAR		12.9g
SODIUM		98mg
KILOJOULES		495 (cals 118)
GI RATING		MEDIUM

Apple and Prune Loaf

SERVES: 12 SLICES

2 small green apples
½ cup seedless prunes
2 egg whites
¼ cup sugar
1 x 200g tub no-fat French vanilla yoghurt
½ teaspoon bicarb soda
¼ cup water
2 tablespoons (30g) Flora Light® margarine melted
2 cups self-raising flour
½ teaspoon cinnamon
cooking spray

Dietitian's Tip
Including fruit in the recipe increased the nutritional composition. This, along with the recipe being low fat, makes it a great alternative to the traditional cake.

DIRECTIONS

Preheat oven 180°C fan forced.

Peel and core apples, then cut into small dice. Cut prunes into small pieces. In a medium size mixing bowl beat egg whites and sugar using an electric beater for 1 minute. Add diced apple, prunes, yoghurt, bicarb soda, water and melted margarine. Combine well. Sift flour and cinnamon into bowl in one go, gently fold mixture until flour is just combined. DO NOT BEAT as this will make the loaf tough. Pour mixture into a large loaf tin that has been coated with cooking spray. Bake 30-35 minutes or until cooked in centre. Turn onto a wire rack to cool.

VARIATION: REPLACE APPLES WITH FRESH PEARS.

Nutritional Information   Ⓕ

PER SLICE		
FAT	TOTAL	1.6g
	SATURATED	0.3g
FIBRE		1.5g
PROTEIN		3.8g
CARBS		24.8g
SUGAR		7.2g
SODIUM		236mg
KILOJOULES		539 (cals 128)
GI RATING		MEDIUM

Cherry Crackles

MAKES: 24 CRACKLES

¼ cup desiccated coconut

3 cups Rice Bubbles®

¼ cup glacé cherries chopped

2 x 55g Cherry Ripe® chocolate bars

1 tablespoon Flora Light® margarine

2 tablespoons golden syrup

1 teaspoon imitation coconut essence

24 paper patty cases

DIRECTIONS

Place coconut onto a sheet of aluminium foil and place under griller, toast until golden brown, be careful as it can burn quickly. Leave to one side. In a large mixing bowl place Rice Bubbles, chopped glacé cherries and coconut, fold together. Roughly chop Cherry Ripe bars then place in a small microwave-safe bowl with margarine and golden syrup. Melt on HIGH for 2 minutes, give mixture a good stir. Add essence to bowl. Pour into Rice Bubbles and fold together until ingredients are well coated. Spoon mixture into 24 patty cases. Refrigerate to set.

Dietitian's Tip
Annette has made a great low fat treat. People with diabetes or on weight management plans are advised to have one and then place the lid on the tin until another day.

NOTE: It is best to keep the crackles refrigerated.

Nutritional Information ®

PER CRACKLE		
FAT	TOTAL	1.4g
	SATURATED	0.9g
FIBRE		0.3g
PROTEIN		0.4g
CARBS		8.3g
SUGAR		5.4g
SODIUM		42mg
KILOJOULES		194 (cals 46)
GI RATING		MEDIUM

Apricot and Walnut Loaf

MAKES: 12 SLICES

2 egg whites

⅓ cup sugar

1 cup carrot grated firmly packed

¾ cup dried apricots diced

¾ teaspoon bicarb soda

¼ cup (25g) walnuts chopped

2 tablespoons (30g) Flora Light® margarine melted

1 x 200g tub diet apricot yoghurt

1½ cups self-raising flour

cooking spray

DIRECTIONS

Preheat oven 180°C fan forced.

In a large mixing bowl beat egg whites and sugar for 1 minute using an electric beater. Add all other ingredients except the flour and combine well. Sift flour into bowl in one go and gently fold mixture until flour is just combined. DO NOT BEAT as this will make the loaf tough. Pour mixture into a large loaf tin that has been coated with cooking spray. Bake 30-35 minutes or until cooked in centre. Turn onto a wire rack to cool.

Dietitian's Tip
Dried apricots are high in vitamins and fibre and have a low glycaemic index. It is great to include them in recipes suitable for people with diabetes.

VARIATION: FOR A LOWER FAT COUNT OMIT WALNUTS.

Nutritional Information ®

PER SLICE	WITH WALNUTS	W/OUT WALNUTS
FAT TOTAL	3.3g	1.5g
SATURATED	0.4g	0.3g
FIBRE	1.9g	1.7g
PROTEIN	3.9g	3.5g
CARBS	22.6g	22.5g
SUGAR	9.6g	9.5g
SODIUM	225mg	225mg
KILOJOULES	566 (135 cals)	491 (cals 117)
GI RATING	MEDIUM	MEDIUM

Symple Cookies - RECIPE 1

MAKES: 24 COOKIES

1 egg white

⅓ cup sugar

¼ cup skim milk

½ teaspoon vanilla essence

4 tablespoons (60g) Flora Light® margarine melted

1½ cups self-raising flour

cooking spray

Preheat oven 180°C fan forced.

Dietitian's Tip
Not much in nutritional value but is low in fat and kilojoules. Can be included in the eating plan of a person with diabetes on special occasions.

Coconut Cherry Cookies

FOLLOW COOKIE RECIPE 1 AND ADD

1 teaspoon imitation coconut essence
½ cup glacé cherries chopped
½ cup desiccated coconut

DIRECTIONS

In a medium size mixing bowl beat egg white and sugar for 1 minute using an electric beater. Add milk and essences to melted margarine, pour into bowl. Add cherries then fold flour into mix until ingredients are combined. Roll twenty four heaped teaspoons of mixture into coconut then place onto flat baking trays that have been coated with cooking spray. Dip a fork into boiling water then press the cookie dough flat (this stops the dough from sticking to the fork). Bake 20-25 minutes or until golden brown.

Peanut Cookies

FOLLOW COOKIE RECIPE 1 AND ADD

2 tablespoons crunchy peanut butter
¼ cup (25g) peanuts chopped

DIRECTIONS

In a medium size mixing bowl beat egg white and sugar using an electric beater for 1 minute. In a small bowl combine peanut butter, milk, essence and melted margarine, pour into egg mix and stir together. Add chopped peanuts then fold flour into mix. When combined spoon twenty four heaped teaspoons of mixture onto flat baking trays that have been coated with cooking spray. Dip a fork into boiling water then press the cookie dough flat (this stops the dough from sticking to the fork). Bake 20-25 minutes or until golden brown.

Sprinkle Cookies

FOLLOW COOKIE RECIPE 1 AND ADD

⅓ cup hundreds & thousands

DIRECTIONS

In a medium size mixing bowl beat egg white and sugar using an electric beater for 1 minute. In a small mixing bowl combine milk, essence and melted margarine, pour into egg mix and stir together. Fold flour into mix. When combined spoon twenty four heaped teaspoons of mixture onto flat baking trays that have been coated with cooking spray. Dip a fork into boiling water then press the cookie dough flat (this stops the dough from sticking to the fork). Sprinkle three quarters of a teaspoon of sprinkles over the top of each cookie. Bake 20-25 minutes or until golden brown.

Nutritional Information Ⓡ

PER COOKIE	COCONUT CHERRY	PEANUT	SPRINKLE
FAT TOTAL	2.4g	2.5g	1.3g
SATURATED	1.2g	0.5g	0.3g
FIBRE	0.6g	0.4g	0.3g
PROTEIN	1.2g	1.7g	1.1g
CARBS	11.7g	8.8g	11.3g
SUGAR	5.5g	2.6g	5.0g
SODIUM	75mg	82mg	74mg
KILOJOULES	303 (cals 72)	272 (cals 65)	255 (cals 61)
GI RATING	MEDIUM	TOO LOW TO SCORE	MEDIUM

Symple Cookies - RECIPE 2

MAKES: 24 COOKIES

1 egg white

⅓ cup sugar

4 tablespoons (60g) Flora Light® margarine melted

1 cup Special K® cereal crushed

1½ cups self-raising flour

cooking spray

Preheat oven 180°C fan forced.

Dietitian's Tip
Not much in nutritional value but is low in fat and kilojoules. Can be included in the eating plan of a person with diabetes on special occasions.

Pecan and Cinnamon Cookies

FOLLOW COOKIE RECIPE 2 AND ADD

¼ cup skim milk

1 teaspoon cinnamon

⅓ cup (40g) pecan nuts chopped

DIRECTIONS

In a medium size mixing bowl beat egg white and sugar using an electric beater for 1 minute. Add melted margarine to milk, pour into bowl and combine. Place Special K into bowl with cinnamon and mix ingredients together. Fold flour into mixture, when combined spoon twenty four heaped teaspoons onto flat baking trays that have been coated with cooking spray. Dip a fork into boiling water then press the cookie dough flat (this stops the dough from sticking to the fork). Sprinkle a little chopped nuts over top of each cookie. Bake 20-25 minutes or until golden brown.

Christmas Cookies

FOLLOW COOKIE RECIPE 2 AND ADD

½ cup fruit mince (in jar)

1 teaspoon mixed spice

DIRECTIONS

In a medium size mixing bowl beat egg white and sugar using an electric beater for 1 minute. Pour melted margarine and fruit mince into bowl, combine. Add Special K and mix well. Fold flour into mix, when combined spoon twenty four heaped teaspoons onto flat baking trays that have been coated with cooking spray. Dip a fork into boiling water then press the cookie dough flat (this stops the dough from sticking to the fork). Sprinkle mixed spice lightly over each cookie. Bake 20-25 minutes or until golden brown.

Lemon and Date Cookies

FOLLOW COOKIE RECIPE 2 AND ADD

¼ cup lemon juice

2 teaspoons lemon rind

½ cup seedless dates chopped

DIRECTIONS

In a medium size mixing bowl beat egg white and sugar for 1 minute using an electric beater. Add juice and rind to melted margarine, pour into bowl. Place Special K and dates into bowl and mix well. Fold flour into mix, when combined spoon twenty four heaped teaspoons of mixture onto flat baking trays that have been coated with cooking spray. Dip a fork into boiling water then press the cookie dough flat (this stops the dough from sticking to the fork). Bake 20-25 minutes or until golden brown.

Nutritional Information

PER COOKIE		LEMON & DATE	CHRISTMAS	PECAN
FAT	TOTAL	1.4g	1.6g	2.6g
	SATURATED	0.3g	0.3g	0.3g
FIBRE		0.8g	0.6g	0.6g
PROTEIN		1.8g	2.0g	1.9g
CARBS		13.3g	15.2g	10.9g
SUGAR		5.5g	7.3g	3.1g
SODIUM		91mg	99mg	92mg
KILOJOULES		304 (cals 72)	335 (cals 78)	311 (cals 74)
GI RATING		HIGH	MEDIUM	MEDIUM

Index

If you would like Annette to come and speak at your group, conference or seminar please phone:

The Symply Too Good To Be True Hotline (07) 5445 1250 (Int: +61 7 5445 1250)
Annette's Web Site - www.symplytoogood.com.au

Annette's cookbooks are sold in all good newsagents throughout Australia.

For information on stockists phone/fax the hotline or email: asym@bigpond.net.au

THREE EASY ORDER METHODS AVAILABLE

1. Website - secure online credit card orders, Austraila and international
2. Hotline - for credit card orders, Australia and international
3. Mail Order - Australia only. Download order form from website or ring the hotline or email for current price list. Send cheque or money order payable to: Annette Sym PO Box 833, Buddina, Qld 4575. Allow 7-21 days for delivery. Don't forget to include your mailing address.